Don't Be A Dumbass Criminal

Understanding the Laws
and
Knowing Your Rights

by

Krystal Banks

Don't Be A Dumbass Criminal
By
Krystal Banks

ISBN: 978-0-69291651-3

CreateSpace Title ID: 7865416

Cover design by: Miles Dixon

Edited by: Gloria Palmer
                  (movinonup57@yahoo.com)

Fourth Printing: January 2019

Table of Contents

Before you get into this book,
I need you to understand about
SNITCHING ON YOURSELF:

YOU NEVER NEED TO ANSWER
ANY POLICE OFFICER'S QUESTIONS—
EVEN WHEN YOU ARE CAUGHT IN THE ACT!

MOST PEOPLE DON'T REALIZE
THEY ARE TELLING ON THEMSELVES,
AND **YES**,
EVERYTHING YOU SAY IS A STATEMENT!

YOU'VE JUST TOLD ON YOURSELF.

1. Introduction

I wrote this guidebook to help anyone to easily understand the court system. If you don't understand the system, you can get ripped off. The fact that you don't live "that life" and you've never broken the law doesn't mean anything. While you probably think you will never get in trouble, you still need to read this book. Better safe than sorry. I wrote this book because I want people to know there's a big difference between what you see on television and real life. Television is for entertainment. This book is about giving you information that could be the difference between your freedom and a life sentence.

Scams happen to people every day. Sadly, people still think the system is fair. It's also sad that people can go through the system several times and still not understand it. Criminals think because they've gotten in trouble before, they know what they're doing. Hey, dum-dum, if you'd learned the first time, you wouldn't be going through this again.

I was tired of people not understanding how to sue someone and win. The court clerks **CANNOT** help you. I hear people complaining about how they didn't get a fair trial and don't know why. It's because the system is stacked against you. That's why it's important understand what-the-heck is going on. I've had a ton of clients who got convicted because they didn't know what they'd signed. All they were told was, "Sign here and you won't go to jail." Later, they found out they could have gotten a sentence that wouldn't have stuck on their record in the first place. I've had clients who couldn't read, so they just nodded their heads and signed.

I wrote this book with help from attorneys, judges, police officers, and several friends. I got tired of seeing people not understand the system. Crime is not just in "the hood". People sound dumb saying crime doesn't happen in their area. Yes, it does! You just ignore it. Privileged America is going away. Crime is happening everywhere. People don't talk to attorneys to ask about crime and whether it's really getting worse out there. They call attorneys when they need them and only ask questions specific to their issues.

This doesn't apply to all attorneys, but I started seeing that attorneys weren't taking the time to explain in layman's terms (non-professional words) what was happening in people's cases and how it would affect them in the future. In most cases, you must take the initiative to research the laws and ask other attorneys questions about your case, so you and your attorney don't miss anything on your case. The more questions you ask your attorney, the better off you will be. These attorneys were using the line of, "I told you. It isn't my fault you didn't understand it. You should have told me you didn't get it." Ask that attorney: "Is this what you would do for your child?"

But, you signed it, and now you don't know where to go get it changed. Or, if you can get it changed. In some cases, you can. So, if no one is explaining the real deal to you, you're falling for a bunch of mess. The trump card is called *Proxy Nunc Pro Tunc*. It's a Latin term that means to go back in time and change your conviction.

What person do you know who calls an attorney before they commit the crime and says, "What happens if I get caught doing this crime?" Most attorneys aren't going to tell you what's going to happen. That's how they make their money—off dumb criminals.

Do you know people who do their jobs every day, but don't know the loopholes? If a person doesn't know the rules, how will they be able to get around them? I talk to people every day who have no clue they are breaking the law. You need to have a clean record if you want to be successful in life, and having a crime on your record will only make your life harder.

If you are ever arrested, the first thing you need to know is *KEEP YOUR MOUTH CLOSED!* It isn't about what the police/prosecutors know. It's about what they can prove! *MAKE THEM PROVE THEIR CASE! DON'T HELP THEM DO IT.* Don't fall for the line, "If you're innocent, you have nothing to hide!" *WRONG!* Whether you're innocent or guilty, calling an attorney should be your *FIRST* line of defense! Don't try to explain your side of the story.

ONCE YOU ASK FOR AN ATTORNEY, KEEP YOUR MOUTH CLOSED AND WAIT FOR YOUR ATTORNEY! ONCE YOUR ATTORNEY IS THERE AND YOU TELL THEM WHAT YOU'VE DONE, THEY WILL ADVISE YOU WHETHER YOU NEED TO KEEP QUIET OR TO NEGOTIATE A DEAL IN ORDER TO HAVE A BETTER OUTCOME. REMEMBER, THEY ARE THERE TO HELP YOU, NOT YOUR CO-DEFENDANTS.

We are taught the system is fair. If we lived in a perfect world, maybe that would be right, but the truth is, we are human and we make mistakes. Knowing that, the system can't be fair. It will work for some, but it won't work for all. It depends on what side you're looking at the system from. In this book, I try to get you to understand both sides. The system wants us to think it is set up to give everyone a chance and you are innocent until proven guilty. That is totally wrong. If you go into a situation thinking you're going to get the benefit of the doubt, you will lose.

You must know the truth to understand this book. The system is designed for rich criminals who can afford to pay for good attorneys and other services that will get them off. This is the same system that was designed for poor people to go to jail because they can't afford to play the game. No money means paying your debts with your time. Understanding this will help you with any case you might have because now you're looking at the law for what it is: a system that's built on money. Knowing the system is built on money means knowing justice can't be fair. With this in mind, that makes the whole system backwards: You aren't innocent until proven guilty; you're guilty until you prove your innocence. That's why the system actually works.

People don't understand how important it is to have a good attorney—which is not necessarily an expensive attorney. The reason the court-appointed system doesn't seem to work is because the State can't pay the attorneys for the resources they need to fight your case.

The first thing an attorney is taught is to never ask the client if they're innocent or guilty. The reason they're taught this is so they can provide you with the best defense regardless. Some attorneys will not represent you if you are charged with certain crimes due to their personal beliefs. Other attorneys will represent you because they know the facts in this case don't line up— even though they know you are dead-guilty of a crime, but you're being overcharged. Meaning, you may actually be *guilty of a crime*, but you're *innocent of the crime you're charged with*.

You need to know some attorneys will fight harder for you if they feel you are innocent. Sometimes, they will even provide you with some services at a reduced fee or no fee because they truly believe innocent people should not be in jail. Some attorneys will cease to represent you if they find out you lied to them.

The faster you realize what type of attorney you need, the better you are. A good attorney is not always going to be the most expensive one. You need to know it isn't just knowing you're innocent, but proving your innocence by legal standards. Knowing this means tell your attorney the truth because, if they know the whole truth, they will know when the prosecutor, witnesses, and detectives are lying.

You have to remember: the detectives and prosecutor only look at the case from their point of view. They don't necessarily know the truth. They just believe the witness is telling the truth. A decent defense attorney will look at both sides of the case and have a pretty good idea what the other side is planning. They will know the best way to present your case, considering all the facts, to hopefully win your case. That's why it's so important that you tell your attorney the truth.

Find an attorney who is going to fight for you! An attorney's job is not to prove your innocence. His job is to protect your rights and provide a credible defense to the prosecutor's charges. Sometimes innocent people need a private investigator more than an attorney to research the facts and provide the evidence to refute the prosecutor's charges. So, if you have an attorney and you are completely innocent, and they just don't believe you, or they keep offering you plea deals, get another attorney. The case has to fit the lawyer, not the lawyer needs to fit the case.

You may need a specialist or you may need a seasoned attorney if you have a serious case. Court-appointed attorneys get paid much lower fees than a hired attorney, and they won't have the resources you might need to win your case.

The system can be double-sided when it comes to people who get accused and charged with a crime. Sometimes, the facts make the situation look one way, and depending on the detective doing the research, you can get a detective who jumps the gun and doesn't find all the facts on both sides before they move to the next step. Is it their job to find all the facts to do their job?

Unfortunately, the system is built so the complaining person (the one who's making the accusations) is the only one who gets heard in the case for several months. What that means is, if someone calls the police department and makes up a lie on you, the police can and probably will arrest you and charge you without any questions because the person making the complaint is considered to be an honest person. It's very unfortunate if you are the innocent person. One-sided stories can make even an innocent person look very guilty.

Then, to fight the case can be very costly. The system is set up to make the accused person look guilty. You ask, how? Easy; because for the first several months of the case, the only side heard is the prosecution's. The judicial system believes that side of the story because it has gone through the steps to find something a person has supposedly done to charge them. This is one of the reasons the judicial system has a 95% conviction rate.

In many cases, it may be cheaper and easier to take a deal rather than fight the case because it does cost more to prove your innocence. The justice system can be scary, but you can't be so scared that you don't fight for your freedom. Sometimes, if you fight your case, you can still lose, and the punishment will be worse than the deal they offered you; so understand all of your options. People truly need to understand their situation because taking a plea for something you absolutely did not do is unfortunate, and it shows how broken the system is.

What people also need to know is you can sue. Yes, it can be hard to sue the police, or perhaps the judicial system or the county, but it can be done. In certain cases, the prosecutor will go after the person who lies by falsifying a police report. But you will have to fight for this.

It is a very sad to have to teach people how to speak or act with the police, but in today's society, respect is clearly not being taught. Common-sense issues are being violated. When have you ever seen being belligerent work in society? We now must teach people to be courteous to one another. Speak clearly. Don't yell. Don't have an attitude. And, *NEVER* run from the police.

Law Abiding Citizens vs. Criminals

Law abiding citizens don't worry about the law. They work, stay busy doing positive activities that help the community, and mind their own business. They live a basic life and generally have had very few, if any, encounters with the system. Knowing right from wrong is based on four general rules:

1. Stay away from drugs.
2. Absolutely *NO* violence.
3. No stealing.
4. No cheating.

When you live by these rules, you won't have to worry about the law.

Criminals don't think about the law. They worry about themselves, They are only trying to help their situation out by taking a shortcut. They are so busy planning a quick move that they forget how the system works and that's why they get caught. They don't think about who's watching or who it will affect. They don't care if it's right or wrong until they get caught. Then they want everyone to feel sorry for them because they got caught doing what they had no business doing in the first place.

When you live by no rules, you will have more than enough time to learn from your mistakes in prison.

Excuses About the System

The system wasn't set up to target race! It was set up to make money; so, if you don't have money, you won't have a chance with the authorities.

Stop using poverty as an excuse to break the law. Being broke *DOES NOT* give you the right to commit a crime. Find another way! Even though you didn't get caught doing the crime the first, second, or third time, you're still breaking the law. Eventually, you will get caught. It's just a matter of time!

♦♦♦

2. Understanding the System

How the System Is Set Up to Work

The system is supposedly set up to protect the innocent. What that is supposed to mean is, if you don't break the law, a police office, prosecutor, or judge will not be able to sign a warrant to charge you with a crime. Most people in the world are law-abiding citizens, and innocent people believe, if they didn't do anything wrong, the system won't fail them. However, whether you are innocent or ignorant (committed a crime but didn't realize you were committing a crime), you must accept the fact that you are being charged with a crime, and you must get prepared to help your attorney provide a defense.

On the other hand, the judicial system has a 95% conviction rate in cases where people were charged with a crime. Do you want to know why? It's because the system is set up to charge people when there's enough evidence that a crime has been committed.

See, the system tells us we are innocent until proven guilty. I hate to say this, but that isn't true. When a crime has been committed, the police recognize something has happened and something is wrong, so they begin to try to understand what happened. Once they put the pieces together, they take their story and some type of evidence to the prosecutor. Then the prosecutor goes to a judge, who signs a warrant.

So now we have been through 3 different channels to see that a crime has been committed. The police, the prosecutor, and the judge assume this person is guilty of a crime. Sometimes, it may not actually be the crime the person is being charged with, but they feel there's most-certainly evidence of a crime. That's called overcharging.

They only charge you when they think they have you red-handed.

EXAMPLE: Someone didn't want to give you the money they owed you and they go complain to the police. The police can charge the person with armed robbery. That charge doesn't necessarily mean you had a weapon or touched someone. It could simply mean the person felt some kind of way about handing the money over to you. Maybe they changed their mind about the money. We would look at this as a messy transaction, but the court may not know all the details, and until they find them out, there is a crime that is going to be prosecuted. Regardless of how things really happened or how they look, you still could get convicted.

In this type of situation, everyone knows something is wrong. Now it's time to prove it, so you want to hire a real attorney, and real attorneys represent real criminals. You know, the criminals who know and admit they did something wrong, but they still want you to get them off. The most important thing you can do is tell your attorney the *WHOLE TRUTH*!

A real attorney is going to need the absolute truth because their job is to take the people who are supposed to be telling the truth (police officers) and catch them up in their small lies. That is how the really good attorneys get you off. Real attorneys don't give a crap if you're innocent or guilty. See, no one in the court thinks the dum-dum sitting next to their attorney is innocent— including the dumb criminal who told their attorney yesterday they did the crime. And the criminal will have the nerve to say, "What should I plea?" Hello, dummy, your stupid-butt needs to stand mute and let your attorney do their job. Their job is to provide a credible defense to the prosecution's charges. If they can't do that, their job is to try to negotiate for a charge that may fit what your actual crime was. Remember this:

- The court is a business. It's set up to make money.

- The court and government are made up of attorneys. These same attorneys make the rules and get paid well for it.

- The system is designed so these attorneys who create the laws will get paid, and attorneys want other attorneys to get paid, so don't be shocked.

- With that in mind, there is absolutely NO attorney willing to give you free advice. Even if you *think* it's free, you will pay later. They will give you just enough information for you to come back and hire them later.

- Asking an attorney for free advice is like asking an attorney about a crime you're thinking about committing. Do you really think they're going to tell you what laws you're going to break and how much time you'll get without getting paid? NO! They won't tell you the truth—until after you commit the crime, so they can charge you to try to get you off.

- The court system is in everyone's pockets.

- Even if you're found not guilty of a crime, you will have paid a lot of money for bail and attorney fees that you don't get back.

- The costs are expensive, even if you're innocent.

- If you pay a bail bondsperson, you don't get your money back.

- If you fight an insurance ticket, you will still have to pay a fee just for getting a ticket that was dismissed.

- No attorney is going to make a judge angry over your case so that judge can mistreat them or another client of theirs later.

- Why doesn't the justice system go after criminals who are out of state? The costs!

- Not knowing the law will still get you a case. Ignorance of the law is no excuse. It is your job to learn the law. The excuse that you didn't know you were breaking the law won't work in court.

- Stop trusting other people with your life. Everyone is **NOT** on your side. Even though we've been taught to trust the police, they can and will lie to you.

- You had better start doing your own research. Start questioning everything during and after the case is over.

- All counties have extradition budgets. What that means is, they may not be able to afford to pay for you to be brought back to court, depending on the seriousness of the crime. For example, they may only budget for bringing violent offenders back. That isn't to say they won't bring back drug offenders, but it may be less likely.

- Even though we've been taught to trust the police, it is their job to find out what really happened and to prosecute you. They aren't on your side. They're on the side of justice.

- When people say, "I plead the Fifth," what do they mean? The Fifth is your Fifth Amendment right that means you don't have to say anything because, if you do, you might be telling on yourself. Don't talk too much. This is your right when talking to authorities.

● ● ●

3. Quick Guide on How the Court System Works

A. When a crime is committed, someone contacts the police and is assigned a detective. (They must complain and want justice.)

B. They tell the detective what happened, then write out what happened (give a statement).

C. They must provide some type of proof of the crime (evidence).

D. The detective does an investigation, writes up a Complaint, and sends it to the prosecutor.

E. The prosecutor reviews the Complaint and the evidence. If they have enough evidence to charge a person with the crime, they issue a Warrant. (There needs to be enough proof to show a crime has been committed. The more proof they have, the easier it is to get a Warrant.)

F.   The Warrant is entered into a national database.

G.   The "criminal" is arrested.

H.   In most cases, the criminal must be formally charged (arraigned) within 72 hours of the arrest, or released. If the arrest is on a holiday, it may be 96 hours. This is when bail, if any, is set.

I.   This is when you contact a bail bondsman—after you get arraigned. Their job is to discount the amount of money the court wants for you to get out of jail. Then you get an attorney.

J.   If you file a Complaint against someone, you need to understand that, even if you are lying or change your mind, it will still cost money to hire attorneys to clear the issue up, not to mention how much it may have cost to investigate. Then, it can turn into a charge of filing a false police report and that is a serious charge. Dropping the charges is not as easy as it sounds. The court system puts a lot into investigating cases.

K.   When a Complaint is filed, someone wants justice. There may be witnesses. Witnesses always tend to pop up in cases.

NOTE: People don't just get arrested; the police aren't just trying to pick on you. Most of the time, you just finally got caught.

Getting Bond

1. A judge or magistrate has to formally charge you (arraignment).

2. They look at:

    a. your past record (which includes not showing up in court for tickets);

    b. the crime itself—whether there is Probable Cause a crime was committed;

    c. your ties to the community (do you have a job, do you rent or own, how long at your house);

    d. the safety of the public—to determine what it will take to make sure you go back to court.

Bail vs. Tether

1. The court makes money off tethers.

2. Bail: Pay up to a 10%, one-time fee.

3. Tether: Pay a $360 fee up front, then around $10 a day—so approximately $310 monthly.

3. Example: $5,000 cash/surety bonds:

    a. Pay $500 to bail bondsman, or

    b. Pay $5,000 to the court.

4. Is it really worth your attorney asking for you to be on a tether? Weigh your options.

5. Does a tether (ankle bracelet) really stop you from breaking another law? No! But, even though the accuracy of a tether may not be precise, the tether's GPS will register within a specific area that is close enough to prove you were in the area where the crime was committed.

♦ ♦ ♦

4. The Court Process

A. Every process starts in District Court, whether it is a misdemeanor or a felony.

  1. Arraignment: The court tells you what you are being charged with, then gives you a bond. A bond is supposed to be to make sure you show up to all your court dates, but some judges will use it as a punishment. Is it fair you're being punished before you're even found guilty?

  2. Preliminary Exam: One of the most important court dates. You want to know why? This is where the prosecutor must show some of their evidence (just enough to get to the next stage) and they have to prove it (where you can get the charges dropped).

      If they don't have enough evidence to prove Probable Cause, your case can be thrown out (dismissed). If they do have enough evidence, you either try to work out a plea deal or you get bound over to Circuit Court, if your case is a felony, where the above steps are repeated and your bond can be raised or lowered. If your case is a misdemeanor, it stays in District Court and proceeds to trial.

The duty of the prosecutor is to seek the truth, not to seek a conviction. Sometimes the court system can seem like they are playing a game because it gets to be about wins instead of justice. This is why the prosecutor's job is to seek the truth because that can lower your charges. It isn't about the prosecutor fighting with the defense or the judge. It's about the truth!

You need to understand why your attorney may want to waive your Preliminary Exam. The exam may allow the witness to make a statement that is now on record that will hurt your case in the long run. That is why it is important to know when to waive your Preliminary and to have a very good attorney. You don't want it to backfire.

3. Plea Hearing: To work out a deal.

4. Trial:

    a. Jury Trial: 6-to-12 people get to hear your case and decide if you are guilty. Remember, they are given rules to follow, but most of the time, they don't use common sense to understand your case. These people don't live in your world and many have never even been charged with a crime, so they will never truly understand your circumstances. **FOR EXAMPLE:** Why you would live in the inner city vs. the suburbs? What are the street rules? These jurors can't seem to put themselves in your shoes, but they need to for you to get a fair trial.

b. Bench Trial: The judge hears your case without a jury and decides your punishment.

5. Sentencing: You get your punishment.

B. Felony Process

1. Arraignment: The court tells you what you are being charged with, then continues your bond from District Court, or they can change your bond. That means they can raise or lower it.

2. Pre-Trial Exam: This is where you negotiate, and if you can't negotiate, it goes to trial. Your attorney can ask for an Evidentiary Hearing if they feel there was some constitutional violation.

3. Trial: Same as Trial in Misdemeanor Process above.

4. Sentencing: You get your punishment.

SOME PROCEDURES MAY BE DIFFERENT IN DIFFERENT AREAS OF THE COUNTRY, BUT WILL STILL BE VERY SIMILAR.

5. Court Job Descriptions

Understand what the people do who work in the court system.

1. Defense Attorney: makes sure the court follows the law and works out the best deal for you.

2. Prosecutor: works for court to prove you committed a crime and to protect the public's safety.

3. Judge: listens to both the prosecutor's and the defense attorney's stories. If guilt has been proven (see Jury Trial and Bench Trial above), punishes the criminal. **NOTE:** The judge has the final word and can overturn a jury verdict.

4. Bailiff: makes sure the court stays safe.

5. Detective: checks out a Complaint and investigates to see if the law has been broken.

6. Clerk: files all court paperwork and collects payments. Gives no legal advice.

7. Juror: listens to both sides of the story and decides who is telling the truth. Your responsibility as a juror is to look at the facts and evidence, and decide if they support the charges. It isn't about what you know! It's about what has been proven! Don't overthink it!

8. Magistrate: person who listens to the facts and judges the issues (not always a lawyer).

9. Bail Bondsperson: gets person out of jail and babysits them so they make all court appearances.

10. Tether Company: keeps track of your every movement for a nice price.

11. Pretrial Release: pretrial release personnel check out your past record and report to the judge if it would be safe to release you into the public and you'll come back to court. (It sounds nice to get your loved one out for free, but do you *really* want a criminal out for free who isn't being monitored?)

12. Police: regulate the law and protect your safety.

13. Court Administrator: makes sure court employees are following the court rules.

14. Court Reporter: listens to the case and records everything said in court.

15. Referee: listens to both sides and tries to negotiate a deal.

16. Process Server: locates you and gives you court paperwork.

● ● ●

6. Quick Attorney Facts

Do you really know what an attorney's job is? It is to advise the client; interpret the laws, rules, and regulations; analyze what's going to happen; make a strategy; and hopefully, win your case.

When going to an attorney:

a. Their job is to find out your past record.

b. They are going to ask you what happened and you **MUST** tell them the truth. Your attorney needs to know:

(1) How did you do it?

(2) When did you do it?

(3) Why did you do it?

(4) What did you do with the evidence?

Your attorney needs to know everything to know how to defend you.

People have a misconception about attorneys. They seem to think a less-experienced attorney—or one who charges less money, or one who is not as well-known—won't represent them as well as a more-expensive, more-experienced, more-visible attorney. I see people with a good attorney who is willing to fight for their case because they want and need the win, but that person would rather go into debt to hire an attorney with a bigger name who will do the same thing the first attorney would have done.

If you understand what you are looking for when hiring an attorney, it will help you understand what they are supposed to do for you.

1. Don't just talk to one attorney; talk to several. Hiring the wrong one can get you screwed.

2. Don't hire an attorney just because they tell you what you want to hear.

3. An attorney should be able to look at your case and give you an estimate of what will happen.

4. There are some unethical attorneys out there who will take your money and a-bullshit-case, knowing they won't win, just to make you happy and so you will feel like someone is doing something for you. You need to remember it may just be all about making a quick buck.

5. Hire an attorney who has experience with the type of charge(s) you have.

6. Hire an attorney who is willing to go the distance for you without breaking the bank.

7. Hire an attorney that, if they are unfamiliar with your type of case or deal, they know to ask for help from another attorney. A lot of attorneys will help other attorneys.

8. Basically, you're looking for the attorney who will best represent you for what you specifically are being charged with.

If you need help looking for the right attorney, you can use the free **BANKS BAIL BONDS** app. In the app, push the "More" button.

If you need to know your rights, you can also find them in the ***Banks Bail Bonds*** app.

This is the behind-the-scenes of how the system works:

Sometimes when you pay high attorney fees, part of that is going toward donations for the judges' campaigns, which may cause your attorney to have a better relationship with your judge.

A lot of these attorneys tend to have a lot of cases and advertisements; they dress nice and have nice cars. Don't let this distract you because, depending on what kind of case you have, you may need this type of attorney with the connections to win for you. Some judges like attorneys who beg for their clients. The point is, the attorney's job is to do their best to help their client. Does it really matter how they get the result you need?

Then you have those attorneys who go into the judges' chambers and make deals, but those are usually the pretty good deals—you know, the deals by the law. Every case has to have a back door. It's called the Cobbs Rule. If they don't offer a back door, meaning a lesser crime or plea deal, then one of these behind-the-scene attorneys will bring it to the judge's attention, take the case all the way to the Supreme Court, and make a new law on it. They fight on principle alone, and it generally doesn't matter what the cost is, they will win for their client.

You knowing this means stop turning on the attorneys who make these deals for you because 95% of the time another attorney wouldn't or couldn't get you the deal they are getting for you. After the fact, you can't have the nerve to say, "If you were good, you would have gotten me off." Please! You probably were looking at some serious time and they worked their butts off to get you the highly-impossible deal you did get. Tell your family and friends the truth.

There are a lot of big, expensive attorneys with most of their clients sitting in jail telling people who great their attorney is. If you think about that, you'll see that doesn't make a lot of sense. Why are they in jail? LOL. That's why there are different types of attorneys.

See, in every situation, money talks and bullshit walks, so don't be a fool and get cheap when it comes to your freedom. You can go to prison with a car to come home to and a little bit of money to start up with when you get out, or you could have sold that car and paid your attorney to keep you from going to prison. Priorities!

Remember, knowing is half the battle, so don't be fooled by what it looks like. You want an attorney who wins at all costs, not the one who has a lot of wins and very high costs. If an attorney doesn't like this, they may be one of the rip-off attorneys. There are ethical and non-ethical attorneys. Do some research before you hire an attorney. ***It's your freedom on the line!***

7. Hired Attorney vs. Court-Appointed Attorney

Don't hire the attorney who wins a lot. Hire the attorney who only wins! (The attorneys who only win may not take your case if they don't think they can win and that tells you something!) Plea deals may not be considered a win, but it may be the best deal for you.

Even when you pay for your own attorney, it doesn't always mean they're on your team. Yes, they are supposed to be, but that isn't always the case. An attorney who doesn't do everything he can to refute the charges in your defense or try to negotiate a deal for you is not on your team.

Having a court-appointed attorney doesn't always mean you're getting a bad attorney. You aren't directly paying for the attorney, but they still work for you and it is your job to stay on them—just like you would a hired attorney. Don't let them use the excuse they don't have to do something as small as filing a Motion for a bond reduction or filing a Writ to get you transferred to another court, because that's their job. Plus, you can file a Grievance against them too. A Grievance gets the attorney in trouble.

If your attorney misrepresents your case, you have a reason to appeal your case. (Misrepresents: withholds information like a plea deal; doesn't tell you everything about your case; doesn't file the right Motions for you; fails to ask the right questions or call the right witnesses— which causes you to be found guilty.)

You should always ask questions about your case and it is very important to ask the following types of questions:

1. Have you had any cases like mine? What was the outcome?

2. How is your relationship with the judge and the prosecutor in my case?

3. What do you think will happen in my case?

4. What can I do to help you win my case?

5. What types of plea deals is the prosecutor offering?

6. If I'm convicted, can the charge be expunged later?

7. How much do you charge?

8. I need receipts and a detailed bill of how you are using this deposit. (You can't trust all attorneys with your payments. They are supposed to keep records of your payments. You may have to sue them later.)

9. Have you ever had a Grievance or Complaint filed against you for your services? If so, what happened?

NOTE: REMEMBER, THERE ARE POLITICS IN EVERYTHING, AND RELATIONSHIPS MATTER.

Real talk: It's important to hire the right attorney. That includes: (1) knowing when to hire one in or out of your race who may have better connections; (2) whether to hire a local one or not, because connections are real.

Not thinking about these connections can ruin you case. Do your homework.

NOTE: You can always file a Grievance/Complaint against your attorney with the Attorney Grievance Commission. They will investigate whether the attorney mishandled your case. Don't be afraid. It's free to file.

We all know money talks when hiring an attorney. You never want to hire one just because they have a big name or a lot of advertising. That type of attorney may not be the best one for you!

Tips on How to Hire an Attorney

You may have a serious case where you need to hire an 'A' attorney—also known as the pit-bull attorney—who is seasoned. They are well-connected and respected within the system, and they are expensive. The reason you would need an attorney like this is because you are guilty as sin and/or you are facing some serious time—like a life sentence—and you need their expertise. With an 'A' attorney, the judge and prosecutor already know they'll have a hell-of-a-fight with this case because this type of attorney isn't looking for a deal. They are generally looking for the complete win and a dismissal of the case.

Then you have the "B" attorneys. They have good experience, but aren't as well-connected as the 'A' attorneys. They're working their way up the ladder. They'll probably charge you half the amount the 'A' attorneys charge, but will be able to get the same results as the 'A' attorneys. So, the difference between 'A' and 'B' is the amount of experience they have, their connections, and the price.

Then, the 'C' attorneys may not have any of the connections, but they will fight hard for you because they are trying to get the connections and build a reputation for themselves. They'll probably charge half what the 'B' attorneys charge, and they can come up with good results, maybe not as good as an 'A' or 'B' attorney, but still good, especially for the price.

Now 'B' and 'C' attorneys are recommended for cases where you may be looking at up 15 years. These attorneys may be able to do some serious negotiating for your case. The 'D' attorneys may be considered as attorneys who are just trying to get deals—not really trying to go the distance with the case. You may need them to deal with a ticket or some type of misdemeanor—nothing too big, where your life and a lot of time could be taken from you.

'A' attorneys may charge $10,000-$20,000, plus.
'B' attorneys may charge $5,000-$10,000.
'C' attorneys may charge $2,500-$5,000.
'D' attorneys may charge $750-$1.500.
(These are approximate figures.)

♦♦♦

8. Bail Bond Process

A bail bondsman's job is to ensure the court you will show up in court. A bond is a third-party contract between the court, the defendant, and the surety (bail bondsman). Bail is not a punishment. It is a way to protect the community and to make sure you see the severity of the crime that was committed so you don't commit another crime.

What does a bail bondsman do? They financially ensure you will go to all your court dates.

1. Who is really responsible?

   The co-signer signs a contract telling the bondsman that, if the defendant doesn't show up for court, they will pay the full bond. If they can't pay, they will give up their assets to pay the debt. They are also agreeing to help find the defendant if they become a fugitive.

2. What cosigners don't understand?

   If they hide a fugitive, they will get charged with aiding and abetting—a 2-year felony. They are responsible until the defendant is sentenced.

   NOTE: **YOU** CAN LOSE YOUR VALUABLES/MONEY/PROPERTY FOR A DEBT TO A BAIL BONDING COMPANY.

   EXAMPLE #1: *If bond is set at $10,000 cash/surety:*

   a. You can pay the court $10,000, and they **MIGHT** return $9,000.

OR,

b.   You can pay a bail bondsman $1,000.

EXAMPLE #2:   *If the bond is set at $10,000 cash/surety or 10%*:

a.   You can pay the court $1,000, and they **MIGHT** return $900.

OR,

b.   You can pay a bail bondsman $250. In some states, they have a 10% rule that allows the bonding company to discount the bond more than the 10%.

By law, a bondsman can't charge over 10%. There is no such thing as finance/travel fees. Your bondsperson is supposed to explain how the system works.

Bail bonds is a process where you could post a bond to get a person out of one jail just for them to go to another jail. Most courts don't take you to the other courts to clear your cases all up at the same time.

Unfortunately, if a person leaves the state, the courts can't afford to go after every criminal who leaves the state, so some people never get justice. If the court won't pick up the fugitive from another state, the bail bondsman can't do anything. If you co-signed the bond, you need to tell your bondsman the fugitive is in another state because the fugitive can walk into the police department in the other state to get you off the financial hook with the bail bondsman. And, if it's too far, the fugitive won't have to stay in that out-of-state jail.

No matter how much the bond is, the bondsman pays the full amount of the bond to the court.

EXAMPLE: When the bond is $10,000 cash/surety and the person does not show up in court, the bail bondsman has to pay the full $10,000 to the court for your failure to appear. So bail is easy: It's "*MONEY OR THE BODY*". It can't be both. The whole point of bail is to secure the money to the court if the body isn't there. To get out of paying the full bond, you must find the person and turn them in to a jail or the court. By law, courts and jails can't refuse to accept a person with a warrant or if a bondsman wants to cancel their bond.

●●●

9. Understanding the Police and Warrants

BREAKING NEWS: THE GOVERNMENT JUST GAVE ALL COURTS THE RIGHT TO CHARGE THE HARSHEST PUNISHMENT!

When a detective is working on a Warrant, their job is to try to get as much evidence as they can against you to show a crime has been committed (Probable Cause) to the prosecutor. This is the start of the story that will be told in court in a criminal case. In most cases, a person goes to the police and files a Complaint, telling the police their side of the story. The police then start to collect information by gathering evidence. Once they feel they have enough evidence, they may try to contact the criminal.

THIS IS WHERE IT PAYS TO UNDERSTAND YOUR RIGHTS! DON'T GO IN THERE WITHOUT AN ATTORNEY!

The police will sometimes come at you in the nicest way possible. They will try to sweet-talk you into telling them your version of what happened. That is the **BIGGEST NO-NO!** That's called **GIVING A STATEMENT.** It may not seem like a statement to you, but it is. Most people don't remember their right to **SHUT UP,** or the fact that they don't have to answer anything. For your information, police don't have to read you your Miranda Rights up front, or at this point in time. It's your right not to go in to speak to the police. There is no Warrant for you at this point. Remember, they are trying to get a Warrant for you. Don't hand it to them!

NOTE: WITH WARRANTS, THEY HAVE PRIORITY WARRANTS, WHERE THEY MAY NOT CHARGE YOU RIGHT THEN, BUT THEY WILL COME BACK AND CHARGE YOU. THAT'S WHY SOME PEOPLE GET RELEASED QUICKLY.

What you need to know about your rights:

1. The police are **NOT** your friend.

2. You have the right to remain silent. **USE IT! SHUT UP! DON'T SAY ANYTHING!**

3. Everything you say can and will be used against you in a court of law. **DON'T SAY ANYTHING!**

4. The police record everything you say so they can use it against you, even jail calls. There is nothing you can say that can help you out of this situation, so even if you think you're smart enough to get yourself out of this issue, **DON'T SAY ANYTHING!**

    The police's goal is to not let you walk out the police station a free person. Yes, they *can and will* lie to you. They may try to bully you, but that is a scare tactic to get evidence against you.

5. You have the right to an attorney and they can be present when you are questioned. If you ask for an attorney, the police aren't supposed to continue to ask you anything, but they'll still try.

    An attorney's job is to protect you from saying the wrong thing to the police that they would use against you later. A good attorney will tell you, "Tell me what happened and I'll decide what to tell them for your protection."

6. If you can't afford an attorney, one will be given to you. Most attorneys won't let you make a statement.

    Probable Cause is enough proof that a crime has been committed—*for example:* videos, copies of paperwork, weapons with matching fingerprints, testimonials from witnesses—then they build the story behind that.

    SHOWING IS KNOWING. It isn't good enough to know your rights. You must show you know your rights. Be nice. No arguing. Stay calm, ask what law(s) you have broken, and ask if you're free to go or if you're being detained.

What to Do When Stopped by the Police

Assuming you are completely legit and you have your driver's license, registration, and insurance, you must be able to give it to the police quickly.

1. If you are a passenger and you don't have your identification, you should give the police your name. Do not answer any other questions without a lawyer.

2. Turn your phone on 'record" before the police reach the car.

●●●

10. What You Need to Know About Catching a Case

The first thing people say is, I know not to talk to the police. **THEN THE FIRST THING THEY DO IS TALK.** If it happens to you, please don't say anything—even if you're scared.

What is a friend? A friend is someone you trust with your secrets. Now, you must trust your attorney with your deepest secrets for your case. An attorney can be disbarred and lose their license to practice law if they betray the client. Make sure you ask your attorney what is the minimum and maximum charge for the crime you're charged with.

EXAMPLE: You have a killer who holds his victims hostage and the police can't find the hostages. If the criminal tells his attorney where the victims are, the attorney will lose their license if they tell—even if it saves the hostages' lives. It's called attorney-client privilege (ethical code).

I tell you this because people don't understand **WHY** they **MUST** tell their attorney the truth. One reason is it's cheaper. Attorneys charge by the hour, so if you lie, how long is it going to take and how much is it going to cost for the attorney to get the truth out of you so they can properly fight your case?

If you tell your attorney the complete truth about your case, they can work to get you the best deal. If you tell your attorney half the story, or a story you think sounds good, and you want the attorney to tell this lie, you must understand this: It may sound good to you, but attorneys are trained to look at the holes you don't see. What happens when the other half of your story comes around to bite you in the butt?

EXAMPLE: Say you and a friend go to a person's apartment you recently met to just hang out and play some cards. While you're playing cards, you get into an argument with this person. Not realizing you and that person have the same phone, you grab the phone and storm out the apartment. They come outside, yelling at you, then spray mace in your face. You escape, but in the scuffle, a pocketknife falls on the ground. You get home, realize this isn't your phone, and you toss it. A few weeks later, the police are knocking at your door. You find out you're being charged with a crime.

How does this case look to you? Most people would say maybe a threat and a simple theft charge for taking the phone.

Wrong! You're being charged with armed robbery, and that's a life offense!

An attorney is trained to ask: What was your relationship with this person? How did you get the phone? Did you snatch it out of the person's hand or grab it off the table? Were there any witnesses who saw what happened? Whose knife was it? When did the knife fall on the ground? What did you do with the phone? In getting the answers to these questions, they can break the charge down to a misdemeanor larceny—a charge with a sentence of 93 days to up to 1 year—rather than a life offense.

NOTE: IT'S YOUR STORY AND THEIR STORY; SOMEWHERE IN BETWEEN IS THE TRUTH.

♦ ♦ ♦

11. Jury Duty

We all dread the day we get the Summons from the court saying, we need you for jury duty, but we, the people, have to go. You are picked for jury duty to listen to a story and the person who tells the best story wins. What you need to ask yourself is, "Is that fair?"

Sometimes we need to challenge the system. Everyone in jail isn't guilty. Here are the most important reasons for serving on a jury:

1. We all know someone who has had an unfair conviction.

2. If we don't go, the court system might pick some close-minded person who won't be bright enough to ask the right questions to make a fair decision.

3. Some attorneys pick the wrong type of people for jury duty.

4. The jury will never be a jury of your peers without people like you. It's important to have local people, not outsiders—like city vs. suburbs—who don't understand your local crime. I mean, same age, race, and creed.

5. Relatable people are ones who have been in minor trouble, ones who might think maybe the police officer set the defendant up.

6. You hear the story, know it has holes in it, and it doesn't make sense. You question: Was there a proper DNA or fingerprint test done? Was evidence tampered with?

7. Don't just assume a person is guilty. It isn't what you *think* it is. It's what *has been proven!*

8. Bottom line is, we matter, and we must do the right thing and sit on a jury.

9. Yes, you get paid for jury duty and parking, and you **CANNOT** get fired for missing work for jury duty.

What I want you to know is most jurors (people who serve on a jury) are not your equals. You will see some old people set in their ways on the jury, perhaps some not-so-smart young person, and probably some people who are of a different race who don't fully understand what's happening in your area. This is stacking the jury. This is how the law puts certain people on the panel to judge your fate. I know, not very fair. And when the jury gives the verdict, if you're guilty or don't win your case, they can't even make eye contact with you.

Ask yourself: "Why do they stack the panel with the wrong people to get the convictions they want?" Oh, because the prison system is a big money-making system. You have the right to tell your attorney you don't want a particular person on the jury.

What do you do if your attorney isn't picking the best jury for your case?

- File a Complaint with the Attorney Grievance Commission.

- Give them a copy of your transcript.

- Publish your Complaint on the internet.

- Give low ratings to their business and them personally on Google, Yellow Pages, etc.

- Tell your friends. Knowledge and word of mouth is powerful.

❖ ❖ ❖

12. Suing

Small Claims or General Civil Court

Clerks can lose their job for giving you legal advice. There are no lawyers in Small Claims Court. If you want a lawyer, you must move it to General Civil Court, and yes, you will have to pay for your attorney.

Most people don't even know how to sue someone or how to collect. First, you need to get your evidence together. Yes, text messages can be evidence. Print your text messages, copy your contracts or agreements, bring your tape-recorded messages and pictures that include screen shots—anything that proves your case. Have your witnesses write out what they saw. Make a copy! People tend to forget what they saw and/or said. Without your proof, you will most likely lose your case.

You'll need to have the person's name, address, phone number, date of birth, and eventually, their social security number, place of employment, and a list of assets. You need to explain how and why they owe you money. Once you win and get your judgment, you will need their personal information for the courts to repossess their items.

Filing A Claim

For small claims, you need an *Affidavit and Claim Form*. It's about $1 at the court.

You can also print the forms from online, but you need 4 copies for court.

Filing Fees (subject to change)

♦ Damage claims up to $600: $25 filing fee.

♦ Damage claims over $600 to $1,750: $45 filing fee

♦ Damage claims over $1,750 to $5,500: $65 filing fee

♦ General Civil Claim - Damage claims over $5,500: $150 filing fee

There is an additional $5 fee for electronic filing.

Fill out the form, giving the reason you're suing and a breakdown of how much you're suing for. You need to prove your damages, so no random amounts. Have some type of detailed list of what is owed.

You can hire a process server or have a friend take it to the person and hand-deliver it—*yes!* put it in their hand—then take the other copy back to the court. Remember, no lying. They can call that person in to testify that they really served the paperwork.

Once you prove your case, you receive a Judgment. You must wait 21 days; then you can go back to the court and file a Writ of Garnishment to take their taxes or paychecks, garnish their bank accounts, or you can file a Seizure of Property to take their personal property for the debt that is owed. Their property will be auctioned so you can get the money, or you can request to keep the property.

Judgments are only good for 7 years. You can file for an extension, but you must do it **BEFORE** the 7th year is up.

If they file bankruptcy, you need to file an Extension on Judgment so you can still collect. If they didn't include your Judgment in the bankruptcy, you can still collect.

If you sue someone and win, they have 21 days to appeal the magistrate's decision, whether they show up in court or not. What that means is, if they file a motion saying the amount is unfair, it will generally go to a judge. A judge will hear the case all over and can make changes to this case, lowering or raising the amount.

What you need to understand at this point is you may need witnesses to testify for you, and you will have to prove every aspect of your case over again. Then, the judge will render a decision. If you aren't happy with that decision, you can't file an appeal because the judge has the final say, but you can file a motion for reconsideration. If the judge changes his ruling, you must ask for the judgment to be in effect immediately. Otherwise, you have to wait the 21-day period. And, while you're there in court, get all pertinent information to collect on your suit, i.e., place of employment, social security number, etc.

The person you sued still can request a payment arrangement. The payment arrangement may be granted if they are working, but they will have to explain to the court where their money comes from and list all their assets and their bills. The payment arrangement may be denied if they are collecting assistance because that can't be garnished.

There is always a 21-day grace period for one to start collections. You must ask the judge on record for the personal information of the person you have sued because you can't complete the court forms without a social security number and date of birth. It will be hard to find out where they bank at or work without this information. You need to ask for everything while you are there because trying to get a Debtor's Exam will not always work, especially when they know they owe you. They just won't show up or will avoid being served.

If you ask for the extra information, you can file for a seizure of property, and the court will take their car or other possessions if there aren't any liens and sell it so you can redeem your money. Another tip is, if someone is on social security disability, unemployment, or some type of assistance, you can't garnish their income. But, if they work an under-the-table job, you can report them. You may want to tell them this because this may give them a reason to pay you rather than lose their income.

Extensions on Judgements and Beating Bankruptcy

People often don't know a judgment is generally good for 7 years, but if you haven't collected your money within the 7-year time frame, there are tricks to help. Most people don't realize that right before the judgment expires, you can file a Motion for Extension, giving you another 7 years to collect. Or, if the person you sued files bankruptcy, you still can collect after the 7 years because the judgment will always be good if you extend it.

For more information on tips on collections, sign up for our blog or webinars (see page 108). Don't worry, you will always win.

● ● ●

13. The **Rights You Give Up**

Once you are on probation or parole, there are certain rights you give up and you may not know it. In many states, you can't vote while on probation or parole. In some states, you can't vote if you've been convicted of a felony, regardless of whether you are or are not on probation or parole. You need to check your state. You also give up your right to privacy; for example, your probation officer can search you and your home at any time. This is important to know when you are trying to say the police are violating your Fourth Amendment (Search and Seizure) rights. When you are talking about searching and seizing, most people only think about warrants.

Warrants are important to understand because many people commit additional crimes by making assumptions about how they work. Then they do things that make their situation worse. *For example:* They know they don't have a driver's license, but they still choose to drive. Then, when the police get behind them, they take off, fleeing the scene, assuming a warrant has been issued, when they could have just stopped and gotten a ticket.

A **Warrant** is a document that gives the authorities the right to search and seize a person or items. This document must be specific—like, correct names, addresses, and what they are looking for—or it is not valid.

An **Arrest Warrant** is a Warrant to arrest you (a person), but depending on the type of crime you are going to be charged with—for example, a violent crime—it may include searching a location to look for you. This warrant is issued so they can charge you with a crime and get you in to custody for court.

A **Bench Warrant** is a Warrant for your arrest that is issued once your case has been started—for example, if you fail to appear in court or you avoid a Subpoena. If you get a ticket and don't show up, or they mail you a court date and you don't appear in court, they can issue a Bench Warrant for your arrest. This type of Warrant is why they pull over so many random cars. They are more likely to find you through a simple traffic stop because they don't have enough police to come to everyone's home. And, if your charge isn't a felony, they can't just come to your home to arrest you on a misdemeanor charge.

A **Search Warrant** tells specifically what the police are looking for and where they can look for it. For example, they have a Warrant to search your apartment. They must have the correct address and the specific apartment number on it. **No typos!** If they have the wrong apartment—like the Search Warrant states "upper" and they needed "lower"—they **CANNOT** search. This also applies when you have been pulled over. They need a Warrant to search your car, *BUT*, if your car smells like marijuana, they can search your car without a Warrant. This gives the police **PROBABLE CAUSE** to search your car.

Driving: When you get your driver's license, you consent to give up your blood, breath, or urine at the request of the police. Driving is not a right; it is a privilege. Police can request that you do a sobriety test. If you fail, they can request a Preliminary Breath Test (PBT). If you refuse to give your blood, urine, or take a PBT, they can get a court order. It is an automatic 1-year driver's license suspension, a $500 fine, and it's a misdemeanor. Therefore, understanding the rules of having a driver's license is important.

If you've never gotten a driver's license and you get a ticket, you need to do the responsible thing and go to court, pay your ticket, then apply for your license. Most people don't know, if you get 2 tickets while never having had a license, you automatically become ineligible to apply for a license for 3 years from the date of the last ticket. What that means is, if you keep driving and getting tickets, you will never be eligible to get a license.

If you have a suspended license and ignore it, a Warrant will be issued because driving while your license is suspended is a misdemeanor that requires you to go in front of a judge.

If you know you have a Warrant, it is your duty to turn yourself in. It looks more favorable to the courts for you to be responsible and walk in, rather than to be arrested and brought in. Most of the time, if you walk into court on your own, they will give you a personal bond because they see you are being responsible.

●●●

14. Misdemeanor vs. Felony

Felonies and some misdemeanors stay on your permanent record. They will not automatically fall off your record. It isn't like your credit report, where things fall off after 7-10 years. You can have some things removed after 3 years for a misdemeanor and 5 years for a felony. Removal from your record is called Expungement. You can do Expungements yourself, but most people hire an attorney because it's easier.

Misdemeanor

A misdemeanor is a minor crime punishable by a fine and/or county jail time for up to 1 year. It is handled in the lower courts, such as Municipal, Justice, or District Court. Misdemeanor punishment is county jail time, not prison. Misdemeanors don't always show up on your criminal background record.

Typical misdemeanors include: petty theft, simple assault and battery, disturbing the peace, drunk driving without injury to others, drunkenness in public, various traffic violations, public nuisances, and some crimes which can be charged as either a felony or a misdemeanor, depending on the circumstances and the discretion of the district attorney.

Felony

A felony is a charge where you get punished for 1 year and 1 day, sending you to prison. A felony means a violation of a penal law of the state, for which the offender, upon conviction, may be punished by death or by imprisonment for more than 1 year, or an offense expressly designated by law to be a felony.

A charge is considered a felony if the offense was punishable by more than 1 year of incarceration; or, when the statutory penalty is not available, if the crime was designated as a felony in the convicting jurisdiction at the time of a prior conviction.

Expungement is the process to remove a misdemeanor or a felony from your record. Getting an Expungement is a privilege, not a right.

If you have more than one felony, you may have to work harder to remove some items from your criminal record. You may want to see if you qualify for the *Proxy Nunc Pro Tunc*—where you can go back in time and change your conviction to perhaps a lesser conviction, taking it down to a misdemeanor. It falls under the interest of justice.

You must get things removed from your criminal record or they will be on your record forever. In some cases, it can't be removed—*for example,* if you have 2 felonies or you have a drunk driving conviction.

Your Past Messing Up Your Future (A Testimony)

It was 1958. I was 18 years old. I got into an argument with a police officer and they charged me with a felony. I spent a couple of days in jail. They told me, if I pleaded guilty, I wouldn't go to jail and everything would be fine. So, what do you think I did? I took the plea. I did have a smart mouth.

Well, I never got into any more trouble, and a few years later, I got hired at Ford Motor Company. I made good money and took care of my family. I got all my children educated and they are living great. For some of my last days, I need a little more help, so they're going to put me into a nice nursing home, but I get denied residency.

Why in the world have I been denied? I have never been denied anything in my life. I have great credit and I'm old. I don't bother anybody. Hell, I'm harmless! How do I get denied? What do you mean, I have a felony on my record and you don't allow criminals in this facility? Well, is there anything I can do? Do you know I had to get that felony expunged off my record?

J. Williams

♦ ♦ ♦

15. Sentencing Guidelines

The class of a crime is determined by the seriousness of the crime and your score:

- Crimes against a person
- Crimes against property
- Crimes involving drugs
- Crimes against public rules
- Crimes that don't keep the public safe
- Crimes that can hurt the public's trust

At sentencing, the court must consider the nature of the crime and the criminal's past, and the sentence must be equal to the seriousness of the crime.

The sentencing guidelines is a scale that rates the harshness of the crime. Important facts may include, among others:

1. The seriousness of the crime.

2. Factors not considered by the guidelines, such as:

   a. The relationship between the victim and the criminal;

   b. The criminal's behavior while in custody;

   c. Does the criminal care or is sorry (shows remorse); and,

   d. Can the criminal can get better with rehabilitation.

The guidelines are a point system that show the court how they may sentence you. Even though you can Google the laws and guidelines, the judicial system makes it very hard for the average person to understand what's going on. That's why you need an attorney to go through the guidelines with you. Usually, there is room for your attorney to negotiate your charge, which would lower your points and give you less time. That's only if you have a good attorney who is willing to negotiate for you.

There are some cases, like drunk driving cases, where the best deal they can get is to let you keep your driver's license and do less than 90 days in jail. Know, of course, on a Drunk Driving 1 charge, you should try to get it reduced to an Impaired Driving charge so you can at least go to Canada. A drunk driving offense is not expungable and you can't go to Canada with a drunk driving offense.

Alternative Sentencing

ANYTHING BEATS GOING TO JAIL! The following is a list of alternative sentences to going to jail.

1. Drug Treatment Program: an inpatient or outpatient drug treatment, or participation in a drug treatment court.

2. Probation with any conditions required or authorized by law.

3. Residential probation.

4. Probation with jail.

5. Probation with special alternative incarceration.

6. Mental health treatment.

7.   Mental health or substance abuse counseling.

8.   Electronic monitoring–a tether.

9.   Jail with work or school release—leave jail only to go to work or school.

10. Participation in a community corrections program.

11. Community service—picking up trash, for example.

12. Payment of a fine.

13. House arrest—you must stay in the house.

14. Diversion—you don't go to jail and you pay a fine. If you don't break the rules, you won't have anything on your record.

15. Home Youth Training Act (HYTA)—a sentence for someone who is under 24 years old, so the charges can come off their record after they have completed their probation and no criminal record will exist. This does not include capital punishment cases or drug offenses.

16. 7411—deferred sentence applies directly to drug crimes.

Yes, some judges will give you HYTA or 7411, and I have seen them given multiple times.

When you wear a tether, there are ways to trick the monitoring system, but if the tether doesn't work properly, what's the point of it?

16. Random Things to Know About the Courts

- Dress Appropriately. The court always wants respect, so **DO NOT** go into court wearing flip-flops, shorts, tank tops, etc. The court might feel this is disrespectful. You may be sent home to change and they can hold you in contempt. So, even if you don't respect them, act like you do.

- Court systems don't talk to each other, so if you have tickets and Warrants in different courts, they won't know about each other.

- Court systems are not instantaneous. It may take days to put information in the system.

- Take advantage of amnesty programs. You won't get arrested and can make a deal on your Warrants and tickets.

- If you get pulled over, politely ask the officer what you did wrong. **NEVER** start talking or admitting you broke any law. You can always use the *non-admittance of guilt* to fight your ticket.

- **NEVER** try to talk your way out of a ticket. Just take the ticket and fight it later. At least you didn't trap yourself.

- Most people claim they know their rights and try to tell the police that too. **IF YOU KNOW YOUR RIGHTS, YOU KNOW NOT TO SAY ANYTHING.**

- Ask the police officer if he gauged you or how he clocked you (speeding offenses).

- Take pictures, if you can, of where you are.

- If you don't have insurance on your car, you can buy it later and present proof of it to the judge for a lesser ticket. Make sure your insurance isn't 7-day insurance. The courts frown on 7-day insurance and it costs the same as 30-day coverage.

- A defense attorney's job is to make sure the courts follow the laws.

What Is a Pre-Sentence Investigation (PSI)?

- It includes: family history, employment history, mental history, criminal history, community involvement, victim statements, and the circumstances of the crime.

- **ALL** jail calls are recorded and can/will be used against you. **STOP TALKING!**

- Guilty or not guilty, you never get your money back— not attorney fees, not bail bonds, not court costs.

♣ ♣ ♣

17.   Did You Know These Are Crimes?

Here are some crimes most people don't know they've committed.

- Picking up someone else's prescription.

EXAMPLE: Jennifer's grandmother had surgery and asked Jennifer to pick up her prescription. Jennifer went to the pharmacy, where she was told she couldn't pick up her grandmother's prescription without her grandmother's identification. She went and got her grandmother's identification, went back to the pharmacy, and picked up her grandmother's Oxycontin prescription.

On her way back to her grandmother's, she failed to yield at a blinking red light and got pulled over. As the police officer was about to give her a ticket, he noticed the prescription bag on the front seat and asked Jennifer about it. Jennifer explained to the officer her grandmother had just had surgery and she had picked up her prescription.

The officer asked Jennifer to step out the vehicle and arrested her. Then, when he looked in the prescription bag, he found her grandmother's identification. Jennifer was charged with two felonies: possession of narcotics and false identification. If Jennifer had only known she needed a notarized power of attorney letter from her grandmother, this would have stopped her from getting charged.

- Giving someone else's name.

- Getting credit in someone else's name.

- Carrying a pocketknife over 3 inches long and certain types of blades—retractables.

- Carrying a taser.

  EXAMPLE: Kim was on *amazon.com* and found a cute pink taser. So, of course, she ordered it and a few others in cute colors for some of her friends. Kim has this taser in the bottom of her purse for months. One day, Kim decides to take a vacation.

  As Kim is going through security at the airport, they see the taser in her purse. They arrest Kim for carrying a concealed weapon. Kim didn't know it was illegal to carry a taser. She just thought it was cute. What Kim needed was a Carrying Pistol License to carry a taser, just like she would need to carry a gun.

- Carrying brass knuckles.

- Offering someone any type of narcotic is illegal— even over-the-counter (OTC) drugs.

- Altering a paper license plate tag.

- Carrying or holding someone else's ID.

- In 2 states (Mississippi and Michigan), it is illegal for a man and woman to get a hotel room together if they aren't married. It falls under adultery.

- Selling and buying food stamps is a felony that falls under Welfare fraud. Social media pages are getting people caught up, but there are other avenues, like going to the grocery store and being recorded using someone else's bridge card. Places like Facebook and Instagram are big areas the government catches dumb criminals who tell all their business.

EXAMPLE: James is a college boy and he's a little strapped for cash, so he gets on Facebook, Instagram, Snapchat, and Twitter, and asks, *Hey, does anyone have any food stamps I can buy?* Some lady replies, *Yes, inbox me when and where I can meet you.* She has 3 kids and she needs some extra cash, but she doesn't know it's illegal to sell her food stamps. They meet up.

Months go by. James graduates with a bachelor's degree in Criminal Justice and has his first interview. He gets the job, passes the drug test, and goes to get his background check done at the State police office... and two officers arrest him. James has no clue what's going on. He's being charged with felony Welfare fraud.

♦ ♦ ♦

18. If You Knew the Difference, Would You Make a Better Choice?

Carjacking: life in prison, 25 years Threat of a person, stealing a car	**vs**	Unlawful Driving Away Automobile (UDAA): 2+ yrs. Same outcome—you stole a car
Carjacking and stealing a car are crimes that will take away your freedom. One bad decision and you could be locked up for 25 years. The risk isn't worth whatever you thought you would gain.		
Armed Robbery: life Threat and taking an item on a person	**vs**	Larceny: 93 days-10 yrs. Taking an item (not on a person)
Drunk Driving: 1 yr. Drunk driving conviction; can't go to Canada any more. Permanently on your record.	**vs**	Impaired Driving: no jail time Lesser charge; and you can go to Canada.

Straight from the Drug Task Force's Mouth

The biggest issue with the drug game is the first few times you get caught, you don't go to jail. The courts give you a slap on the wrist and a fine. What the courts don't tell you is they're building a case against you and they let you think you're getting off easy. But all that case-building will get you in the long run. The more times you get into trouble, the harsher the penalty.

If you have less than 50 grams of cocaine, heroin, or methamphetamines—about the size of a baseball—then, no jail. Because the court lets you off the 1st time—and maybe the 2nd and 3rd times—you start becoming a habitual offender. That's when you will see the time in prison.

Why You Need to Know Something About Your Local Laws

Do you know what a city ordinance is? It's a law for the specific area you're in and it can be broken down as far as a specific zip code. You can actually Google your local city ordinance rules and see what they are if you're thinking about committing a crime. "Why?" you ask.

The government can put a special task force in any area to help the people. Then they use federal vs. state laws to go after people because the federal case has harsher punishment.

Understand your city ordinances; a lot of cities are changing their laws. *For example,* if you go through a 48205 zip code area, which is on the east side of Detroit, and get caught with a gun, it's a mandatory 5 years. They changed it because they considered it to be a very dangerous area. So, even if it's your first time carrying a gun illegally, you're still going to prison for 5 years.

You want to know how they did it? The police, both federal and local, did a zoning change that cracked-down on violent crimes in that zip code. It's called Project 48205. It falls under federal gun laws that are much harsher, with no parole and longer sentences, so it makes violent criminals think twice. A lot of people don't know about this change and some are sitting in prison for 5 years because of it.

Do you know how and why laws are put into place? It's because one group of people want to control another group of people or to control a situation, so they make a law. Laws change or new laws come into effect every day.

●●●

19. New Crimes the Youths Are Committing

If you are underage, you can still be charged as an adult if you commit a crime, or if an adult has you commit the crime. There are courts that have charged youths as young as twelve years old as adults. *JUST KNOW, IT'S YOUR BUTT ON THE LINE.*

How is Bullying/Cyber-Bullying Punished?

IN ADDITION TO THE CONSEQUENCES INCURRED UNDER SCHOOL POLICY, SOMEONE WHO COMMITS AN ACT OF BULLYING MAY ALSO FACE CRIMINAL PENALTIES.

Depending on the specific conduct involved, bullying and cyber-bullying may be prosecuted. The defense to cyber-bullying is free speech and if it's proven it wasn't really a threat.

Stalking

Stalking is usually a misdemeanor, and incurs a fine of up to $1,000, up to 1 year in jail, or both. However, if the victim was younger than 18 years old at the time of the offense, and the defendant was 5 or more years older than the victim, the offense is a felony. Penalties include a fine of up to $10,000, up to 5 years in prison, or both. The judge may also place a person convicted of stalking on probation for up to 5 years, including an order to refrain from contacting the victim during that time.

Aggravated Stalking

Aggravated stalking is a felony, and incurs a fine of up to $10,000, up to 5 years in jail, or both. However, if the victim was younger than 18 years old at the time of the offense and the defendant was 5 or more years older than the victim, penalties increase to a fine of up to $15,000, up to 10 years in prison, or both. The judge will also place a person convicted of aggravated stalking on probation for at least 5 years (up to 10 years), and will include an order to refrain from contacting the victim during that time.

Posting Electronic Messages Without Consent

This offense is a felony, and incurs a fine of up to $5,000, up to 2 years in prison, or both. However, when the crime occurs in violation of a restraining order, when it involves a credible threat to harm or kill the victim (or a member of the victim's family), and in other similar specified circumstances, penalties increase to a fine of up to $10,000, up to 5 years in prison, or both.

Parents should know: If you aren't paying attention to your children, it could cause you to go to jail. If your child is skipping school, **WHETHER YOU KNOW IT OR NOT**, the schools have special truancy officers who can put the parents in jail and charge them with a misdemeanor for their child(ren) missing too much school.

Parents also need to understand: Your child may be getting sexually assaulted at school, and you have the right to press charges. It is a crime for a child to snap another child's bra strap, flash another child, and even try to pull down a child's pants. Even though you may think it's harmless, it is considered sexual assault. Protect your child!

Catch-22 of the Law

What do you mean, they're locking people up for showing evidence?

The law is trying to punish people who video record fights. But, what they don't tell them is, if they video and try to help stop the threat, they won't get charged. On the other hand, if they publish it, they want to charge them with accessory to the crime. Then, if you call the police for help when the crime is being committed, they tell you to stay away and don't get hurt. Which one is it: help or run?

◆ ◆ ◆

20. How to Win Your Case

In a criminal case, it's the prosecutor's job to prove the charges. Most defense attorneys will caution their clients about taking the witness stand, and most defendants who do take the stand do it against their attorneys' advice. The right to remain silent is golden and the jury will be instructed not to use it against you (even though some prosecutors will try to make you look guilty if you don't take the stand). Below are some ways you can help your attorney disprove your case. Intent is crucial in most cases. *INTENT CAN BE THE DIFFERENCE BETWEEN NO TIME AND A LIFE SENTENCE.*

Assault

The prosecutor has to prove you intended to hurt the person. Your defense: it was an accident.

TRUE EXAMPLE: You have your gun license, you're at home, and someone breaks in. You can only shoot the person if they are facing you; you *CANNOT* shoot someone in the back. Why? Because if you shoot someone in the back that means they were trying to get away from you and it shows they were no longer a threat to you. So, if you have a CPL (gun license), you can only shoot if you're in danger.

Carrying a Concealed Weapon

If you're carrying a weapon just to protect yourself, it may look like you were looking for trouble. You must know your open-carry laws or you can get in trouble for concealing a weapon.

Criminal Sexual Conduct

As long as the person isn't underage or mentally challenged, it must be proved you used force. Legal age of consent is 16. Your defense: it was consensual.

Embezzlement

Your defense: you did not steal it for personal gain, or you used the money for that specific business.

Felony Firearm

Your defense: you had no intention of committing a crime.

Possession of Drugs

Your defense: you had no idea you had the drugs, or you have a prescription for the drugs. Just because it was in your car doesn't mean it was yours or you knew about it. Were there fingerprints on the bag of drugs? Was it a newly-purchased car and you had no clue it was hiding in the car?

Receiving and Concealing Stolen Property

If you have receipts from the person you bought the items from, or some type of communication—*for example,* text messages or emails—showing you were buying the items not knowing they were stolen, you can get off. If you bought an item on Craigslist and specifically asked the person if it was stolen, plus you got a receipt for it, you didn't know it was stolen.

Unlawful Driving Away an Automobile (UDAA)

Your defense: you didn't steal the car. Perhaps you were just borrowing it with the intent of returning it, you can get the charge dropped to joy riding. The intent is what gets you. Just like, if you threaten someone while stealing the car, that turns the charge into carjacking and that's a life offense.

Operating Under the Influence (OUI)

The prosecutor must prove you were under the influence. Maybe you barely passed the breathalyzer; maybe you had some type of prescription drug in your system that showed up as a high-alcohol level; maybe the breathalyzer machine was broken and hadn't been calibrated correctly. Did you injure anyone?

Help win your case by thinking outside the box!

You need to understand that **YOU NEED TO DO EVERYTHING IN YOUR POWER** to help your attorney beat your case. That may mean backtracking your steps, asking the neighbors if they have cameras, going to stores to get video surveillance. We understand attorneys are supposed to do this, but your job is to do whatever you can to help because **IT'S YOUR BUTT ON THE LINE!**

EXAMPLE: You play an online game on your phone. There will be some type of IP log of your location.

There are a lot of resources you can use to beat a case; *for example,* video footage on street lights and store cameras. Yes, you'll have to pay for it, but it could save your life. All cellphones have GPS tracking in them, which may prove you weren't in a certain area when you were accused of being there.

EXAMPLE: There was a robbery at a bank that was videotaped. In the video, there's someone who looks like you, but you can prove by the GPS on your phone that you were thirty minutes on the other side of town at the time.

Hey, dum-dum, no matter how you slice the pie, if you break the law, you can't use the law to sidetrack the fact that you broke the law. *For example,* you can't do something illegal, then try to use the fact that you have a legal license. *For example,* you can't carry a gun in a school zone, then say you have a CPL license. It is still an illegal act.

● ● ●

21. Favorable Sentencing Deals

If you get convicted of a crime, there are some favorable sentencing deals. You want to make sure you get this type of deal, and if possible, so the charge can be expunged from your record. You need to ask your attorney, if you take this deal, will you be able to get the charge removed from your record.

NOTE: The goal is not to go to jail and not to have a felony on your record; or, if it is a felony charge, it's one that can be removed. People need to be aware of the probation traps. They add on more serious charges. I've seen probation officers violate people before they were even convicted. What if they beat the case? Or were wrongfully charged? Why do you keep extending the probation? Why are you telling me I can't transfer my probation to a different city?

Types of Sentences

- A defendant may have his or her drug crime sentence deferred only under two special circumstances: 7411 and HYTA (Holmes Youthful Trainee Act).

- What is a deferred sentence? Simply stated, the defendant may avoid a conviction for a drug charge so that his or her public criminal record will not include a black mark for a drug crime conviction. This is possible only if the defendant complies with all the terms of the judge's orders over a specified period of time.

- HYTA (Holmes Youthful Trainee Act): You must be between the ages of 17 and 24 to be eligible for this sentencing. It will be erased off your record.

- 7411: Works with crimes, unlike HYTA, and is considered only for individuals who have never been convicted of any offense in the past. They say 7411 can only be used one time in your life, but that isn't always the case. It applies to the following drug crimes for an individual who is found guilty or pleads guilty:

  - Possession of less than 25 grams of cocaine or less than 25 grams of a Schedule I or Schedule II drug, such as illegal Oxycontin or heroin.

  - Possession of any amount of ecstasy.

  - Possession of any amount of methamphetamine.

- Possession of any amount of a non-narcotic Schedule I or Schedule II drugs, such as GHB.

- Possession of any amount of a Schedule III, Schedule IV, or Schedule V drug—*for example,* illegal anabolic steroids or Vicodin.

- Possession of an analog drug.

- Possession of any amount of marijuana.

- Use of any drug.

- A second charge of use or possession of an Imitation Controlled Substance. This is the one instance under 7411 where a person with one prior drug crime is not excluded from another 7411 sentence. This applies only to prior possession or use, and not to the possession with intent, delivery, manufacture or advertising of Imitation Controlled Substances.

- Diversion. You make a deal to pay back stolen money and it erases the conviction from your record.

♦ ♦ ♦

22. What to Do if You Lose Your Case

If you lose your case, you need to understand this may not be the end for you. Courts and attorneys aren't perfect, so you should study what happened in your case to see if the outcome of your case can be changed. That may include getting transcripts and going over your case line by line, **BECAUSE IT'S YOUR LIFE ON THE LINE!** Actually, do your homework even before your case goes to trial. You can't be lazy and hope someone is going to win your case just because you want it to happen. You must learn how to be proactive and help.

What attorney is going to tell you they misrepresented you or messed up your case? None of them! That's why you must do your own research of the law during your case, and especially after your case if you go to jail or prison. You have the time, and trust and believe, no one cares more about your freedom than you. You're behind bars *alone*—not you and your attorney who messed up. Remember, any misrepresentation can get you a new trial. And, if it happened a long time ago, new laws may be in place to get your case overturned.

There are attorneys who will take your case if your original attorney loses. Where there's a will, there's a way. Your job and responsibility is to know your case to help you see what went wrong the first time. In these cases, when you know what went wrong, another attorney may be able to go another route. And, yes, appeals are time-sensitive, so you must move quickly.

The Appeal Process

If it has been determined the court or your attorney did something wrong or even illegal that caused you to lose your case, this is grounds for an appeal. This is your right and an opportunity to have your case heard before a different panel. You will definitely need an attorney who is passionate about winning this case. In a criminal case, your attorney must have misrepresented you, or withheld important information, for you to be able to get your case re-tried. So, I say to you, make sure you understand what is going on because *IT'S YOUR FREEDOM.*

In some civil cases—if the defense is representing a company that isn't in the same state and the amount is over $75,000—the court will allow attorneys and companies to move your case to federal court. I want you to understand why. In federal court, your jury may not come from your area. They may come from far away. That means they will not be a jury of your peers and they won't understand your situation. They may be prejudice and not even know it. Your case could be in Detroit and they're from the suburbs. They may not understand why you live in Detroit or how you justify your crime because of the area you're from.

There are many biases in the court of law. The court can make an innocent person look guilty just by pointing out where they came from. That's like saying, because you're a certain race, you're guilty or a bad person. Did they look at the facts? Or, were they trying to understand your situation from their point of view and lost track of why they were there?

Distractions in the court are real, but what can you do?

VOTE! We don't vote for federal judges; they are appointed by the presidents. But we do vote for our local District, Circuit, Appellate, and State Supreme Court justices, and also for our local prosecutors. Voting is important and these elections are often overlooked because the public isn't really informed much about how judges and prosecutors think and their backgrounds.

You can get organizations together to hire a lobbyist(s) to make better laws or to change the laws. If a law is unjust, it's your duty to get it changed. What you do can make a difference.

◆ ◆ ◆

23. A Message to Judges and Voters

We respect judges and we need judges to understand: We support your decisions that keep us safe. We also want to keep faith in the judicial system. It is your job to treat people with dignity and speak to them with respect, even though some people may not deserve it. It is your job to be fair and listen to all the facts of the case; then, if the criminal has been found guilty, sentence them according to the severity of the crime within the guidelines of the law.

We need to do more as laypeople in deciding what type of judges we elect into office. Candidates who are running for the judge positions are taking their time to attend our community events and they make time for us to get to know them. We don't value how important this is. This is the time for you to do your research about them and their opponents. Sometimes their opponents are the current judges sitting on the bench. In these cases, you need to ask the current judge what their Expungement record is and how you can verify what they're saying.

One thing very important to the community is to find out if your candidate is fair and if they're for Expungements. This is important because, if you have committed a crime (or, perhaps, a family member has), you need a judge in office who sees you have been a good person, perhaps made some mistakes, but now have changed who you are. As a good, productive citizen, you no longer want your past mistakes to haunt you, and you need them to expunge your criminal record.

Once judges get into office, we don't know how busy their docket is going to be, and it gets pretty hectic trying to reach out to a judge. So, voters, this is why it is important to take advantage of the opportunities to meet your candidates.

The people who are voting these people in most of the time don't get in trouble and may not understand what's really happening out here. Just because the candidate goes to your church or knows people you know doesn't mean they're going to be a good judge. What are they saying they will do for your community? Is the only time you've heard of or from them was when they needed your votes?

Do some research! Go to your city council meetings when the candidates are running and ask these questions of them:

- Are you for or against Expungements?

- What kind of groups are you involved with?

- Are you really involved or do you just pay your dues?

✦✦✦

24. Don't Be A Dumbass Criminal Quiz:
Guess the Prison Time

How much time would you get in prison for these charges?

1. Carjacking?
2. Joy riding?
3. Unlawful Driving Away in an Automobile (UDAA)?
4. Possession with the Intent to Sell Cocaine, less than 50 grams?
5. Possession with the Intent to Sell Crack, less than 50 grams?
6. Possession with the Intent to Sell Heroin, less than 10 grams?
7. Possession with the Intent to Sell Methamphetamines, less than 5 grams?
8. Touching an 18-year-old's butt?
9. Touching a 13-year-old's butt?
10. Unlawful Sex/Oral Sex with an 18-year-old?
11. Unwanted Sex/Oral Sex with a 13-year-old?
12. Snatching someone's purse or wallet?
13. Stealing a new iPhone from a store?
14. Carrying a 3-inch switchblade?
15. Carrying your parent's or a friend's old ID?
16. Stealing someone's iPad out of their house?
17. Kicking someone while in a group fight?
18. Punching someone, breaking their nose?
19. Carrying a taser or brass knuckles?
20. Hiding a friend who's on the run from the law?

(Answers are on page 82.)

25. Criminal Chart

Offense	% of Inmates In Prisons
Drug Offenses	46.3%
Weapons, Explosives, Arson	16.9%
Sex Offenses	8.7%
Immigration	8.4%
Extortion, Fraud, Bribery	6.5%
Burglary Larceny, Property Offenses	4.5%
Robbery	3.8%
Homicide, Aggravated Assault, Kidnapping Offenses	3.1%
Miscellaneous	0.8%
Courts or Corrections	0.4%
Banking and Insurance, Counterfeit, Embezzlement	0.3%
Continuing Criminal Enterprise	0.2%
National Security	0.0%

Top Ten Crimes

1. Drug
2. Assault
3. Driving Under the Influence (DUI)
4. Home Invasion, Larceny, Breaking & Entering, Retail Fraud (HI-LCY-B&E-RF)
5. Carrying a Concealed Weapon (CCW)
6. Carjacking
7. Criminal Sexual Conduct (CSC)
8. Fraud
9. Robbery & Unarmed Robbery
10. Obstruction

26. Crime Time Chart

This is only a guide for the courts to use. Since it is the judge's decision, they can give you less time.

Charge	Per *Attorneys*
Aggravated Assault and/or Battery	1 year
Aiding and Abetting	2-4 years
Animal Cruelty	Up to 6 months
Armed Robbery	Life
Assault w/Dangerous Weapon	2-4 years
Assault w/Intent to Commit Murder	6-10 years
Breaking & Entering Vehicle w/Damage to Vehicle	2-5 years
Breaking and Entering w/Intent	2-10 years
Breaking & Entering w/Intent to Commit a Felony	10 years
Breaking & Entering w/o Intent	5 years
Bribery	8-10 years
Carjacking	20 years
Carrying Concealed Weapon (CCW)	2-5 years
Carrying a Weapon w/Unlawful Intent	2-5 years

Charge	Per *Attorneys*
Checks w/o an Account	Up to 5 years
Computers, Using, to Commit Crime	1-10 years
Child Endangerment	1 year, unless prior, Then 7 years
Child Pornography	2-5 years
Child Support, Failure to Pay	Up to 5 years
Cocaine, Heroin, Methamphetamine < 50 Grams	No jail up to 3 times
Conspiracy	Up to 5 years
Criminal Sexual Conduct 1 (Rape) CSC	Life
Criminal Sexual Conduct 2	15 years
Criminal Sexual Conduct 3	15 years
Criminal Sexual Conduct 4	2 years
Cyber-Bullying	1-15 years w/fine of $1,000-$15,000
Drunk Driving 3	1-5 years
Embezzlement	1-20, depending on amount
Escape from Jail	1-4 years
Fake License Tags	5 years

Charge	Per *Attorneys*
False Pretenses–20,000 or More Attempts	1-6 years
Felony Firearm	Mandatory 2 years
Felon in Possession (of a weapon)	5 years
Financial Transaction Device	1-4 years
Fleeing and Eluding	2-15, depending on degree
Fraud	5-7 years
Hit and Run	1-15, depending on damage
Home Invasion 1	2-6 years
Human Trafficking	10 years to Life
Kidnapping	Up to 20 years
Larceny (Stealing Property from a Person)	Up to 5 years
Mail and Wire Fraud	Up to 20 years
Maintaining a Drug House	2-3 years
Malicious Destruction of Personal Property	1-4 years
Motor Vehicle Unlawful Use	Up to 5 years
Murder	Life

Charge	Per *Attorneys*
Obstruction of Justice	2 years
Operate-License-Allow Person to Operate Up to 2nd Offense	Up to 5 years
Operating Intoxicated/Impaired/ Controlled Substance	1-5 years
Perjury	5 years
Possession of a Firearm	2-5 years
Receiving & Concealing Property	3-5 years
Receiving Stolen Property over $100	6-10 years
Resisting and Obstructing Justice	1-2 years
Retail Fraud 1	Up to 2 years
Retail Fraud 3	Up to 2 years
Solicitation, Child	4 years
Stalking	1-15 years
Theft	1-7 years, stealing goods
Threatening an Official (Police Officer, Judge)	2 years
Treason	Life
Unarmed Robbery	15 years
Unlawful Driving Away Auto (UDAA)	6-10 years

Charge	Per *Attorneys*
Uttering & Publishing	Up to 3 years
Violating Parole, Probation, or Recognizance Bond	2-3 years
Weapons	1-6 years
Welfare Fraud	Up to 3 years
Witness Intimidation	Up to 5 years

*This crime chart is based on first-time offenses. The time on any charge is negotiable. These charges are based on the crime being a felony. Some of these crimes can be broken down to misdemeanors. It is the judge's decision for your punishment. (**THE INTENT OF THE CRIME IS WHAT GETS YOU!**)*

♦ ♦ ♦

27.   Drug Usage Chart

This chart shows how long drugs stay in your system.

Drug	Urine	Hair	Blood	Saliva
Marijuana	15-30 days	90 days	90 days	3 days
Cocaine	5-15 days	90 days	5-15 days	5 days
Heroin	3 days	90 days	1 day	5 days
Ecstasy	2-5 days	90 days	24 hours	5 days
Methamphet-amine	3-5 days	90 days	1-3 days	1-4 days
Molly	2-5 days	90 days	2-5 days	1-5 days

It is important to know the new laws in Michigan about medical marijuana. One law is people under the age of 21 cannot use or possess marijuana. Another law is adults cannot use marijuana in front of a child 16 or younger. It is considered child endangerment.

The next law is you do not have the right to have marijuana or a gun at the same time. It is one or the other. So, if you get caught with a weapon, even though you are open carrying, or you have a carrying pistol license, and you have marijuana on you, you will now be charged with a crime, and vice versa. If you, for some reason, commit a crime and you have marijuana on you or in your system and you have a gun, you will get charged with a crime.

You are not allowed to drive while under the influence of drugs. If you get stopped and you've been smoking marijuana, you will be charged the same as drunk driving. Even though the legal limit for drunk driving is .08, the current legal limit for marijuana in your system is zero tolerance until this State can come up with a limit. You cannot have it in your system and drive, or operate any equipment with it in your system, or you will be charged with operating under the influence of drugs (OUID). The third time, you get charged with an OUID, it is a felony, just like with drunk driving.

- Even if you have a license/prescription to possess marijuana, you must keep it in a locked box when transporting it.

- A lot of employers are now drug testing immediately after an interview, so you won't have an opportunity to go clear any drugs out of your system

✱ ✱ ✱

28. Answers to the
Don't Be A Dumbass Criminal Quiz

1.	20 years	11.	15-25 years
2.	2 years	12.	2 years
3.	5 years	13.	0-2 years
4.	0-2 years	14.	0-2 years
5.	0-2 years	15.	0-2 years
6.	0-3 years	16.	2-4 years
7.	0-3 years	17.	2 years
8.	0-2 years	18.	0-2 years
9.	2-5 years	19.	0-2 years
10.	Life	20.	2 years

29. *Things You Need to Know, Especially if You Don't Break the Law*

Ask yourself: Do you think the police care that you didn't know you were breaking the law? The answer is **NO!** Ignorance has nothing to do with innocence. The point is you did something illegal and now you have to deal with it.

If you have a Carry Pistol License (CPL), there are certain areas where you cannot carry your gun. You cannot carry in a school zone or a courthouse, for instance.

If you have a medical marijuana card, you have the right to buy marijuana and go home to smoke it. You don't have the right to smoke it in your car or at the park. That is illegal and can get you arrested for driving under the influence (DUI) or operating under the influence (OUI).

EXAMPLE: You're illegally parked in a handicapped spot. You're mouthing off to the cop who stopped to write you a ticket. The cop claims he smelled weed. You get arrested for drugs. You should have only gotten a ticket, but you probably didn't know your rights, your window was rolled all the way down, and you didn't even know you gave consent to be searched. You can't say it was racial profiling if you were doing something illegal!

ONCE YOU GIVE YOUR CONSENT TO BE SEARCHED, AN ATTORNEY CANNOT HELP YOU GET THE CHARGES THROWN OUT IN COURT.

If you've never committed a crime, how would you know you're being set up? You wouldn't. That's why you think the law is on your side. LOL. That's why you need to know one thing before answering any questions by anyone: *I NEED MY ATTORNEY AND I'LL WAIT UNTIL THEY GET HERE BEFORE WE PROCEED.*

The more innocent you are, the quicker you need to get an attorney! If you are arrested, even if you have done *absolutely nothing* wrong, it would be wise to ask for an attorney anyway—even if it's just to explain what you know about the situation—because people get nervous and scared and intimidated when speaking to the police. Sometimes, because they are scared, they get confused. You don't want to get in trouble for mixing up what really happened. *REMEMBER: EVERYTHING YOU SAY CAN BE USED AGAINST YOU.*

You get pulled over and you have no clue what the speed limit was. Ask why you were pulled over, then calmly and quietly accept the ticket. *YOU ARE NEVER SUPPOSED TO ARGUE FOR ANY REASON.* If you take the ticket without saying anything else and you decide to fight it in court, you won't be surprised to find out you gave a statement that you didn't realize you were giving *AND* it was recorded.

This goes hand-in-hand with when you're being questioned by the police. Every time, *regardless of whether you're innocent or guilty,* you must know this: *DON'T ANSWER ANY QUESTIONS! KEEP ASKING FOR A LAWYER*

UNTIL ONE IS PROVIDED! Here's how that conversation should go:

- "What's your name?"
  GIVE YOUR NAME. THEN SAY, "I NEED A LAWYER," AND DON'T SAY ANYTHING ELSE UNTIL ONE IS PROVIDED!

- "Do you know what you're here for?"
  "I NEED A LAWYER."

- "If you're innocent, you don't have anything to hide."
  "AM I FREE TO GO? IF NOT, I NEED A LAWYER."

Do you get the point?! You have nothing to say, other than your name, except, **"I NEED A LAWYER."**

I tell people all the time that it is harder to break the law than it is just to follow it, but I realize that may not always be true. The fact that you go to work every day and just go home doesn't mean that somewhere between the two you didn't do something wrong. No matter how small it may seem—*for example,* you didn't put on your seatbelt, or your child didn't have their seatbelt on—it is still breaking the law. No matter how big or small it is, all it takes is one police officer who's having a bad day to pull you over, and you, **MR. OR MS. I DON'T BREAK THE LAW**, could end up in jail.

Many law enforcement agencies have quotas to meet every month. What that means is, every time they give someone a ticket, they get a bonus in their check. That is why they are no longer out here just to protect and serve us. They're constantly out here looking for people who are breaking the law. In agencies where they don't have quotas, if an officer works an 8-to-12-hour shift, how can they justify that there hasn't been anyone breaking the law the whole time they were working? Or, were they really working?

Most officers aren't out there trying to hem-you-up. However, if you get pulled over and don't get a ticket but you get a warning, you need to know the warning goes into a lien. So, if you get pulled over again and you're asked about your driving record, tell the truth. If they check, they will see you have been pulled over previously, but they have the discretion to let you slide again.

Which brings me to, when you're driving and the police are behind you, they generally run your license plate. That will tell them to whom the car is registered, and in many states, if you have insurance. So, it is pointless to give a false name when you get pulled over. "Why?", you ask. In most states, the police system is connected to the Secretary of State's (Department of Motor Vehicles [DMV] in some states) system and they get your picture. Not to mention, you are being recorded, and lying is a charge of resisting and obstructing justice.

Also, it is important to know, if you have unpaid tickets, a Warrant could have been issued for you. If so, they have the right to arrest you. By law, they are supposed to arrest anyone with a Warrant. What you need to know about Warrants is, once you've been arrested, you can be held for 24-72 hours. Depending on what city the Warrant was issued in, however, there is a radius on the area where you can be picked up.

What that means is, let's say the Warrant was issued in Detroit, Michigan, and there's a 30-mile-radius pick up. If you're stopped 60 miles from Detroit, the city in which you were stopped can let you go because they don't have to pick you up. What you need to do after that is make sure you try to take care of that ticket because it can come back to haunt you later.

If you're arrested, you'll be able to use the phone and you can make more than one call. You need to know people's phone numbers because you will not be able to have your cellphone. You also need to know most cellphones are not set up for collect calls, so you may want to know someone's house (landline) phone number.

My company has a free countrywide app called **BANKS BAIL BONDS** *(MobileSoft Technology, LLC)*. It's a free download available at iTunes or the Google Play Store. You put your full name and phone number in. You can  also add up to 3 of your contacts' names and numbers. Then save the information and the button will turn red. Anytime you get pulled over, press the red panic button and it will alert the bail bonds company and your family that you were pulled over, and if you're going to jail, where. It works all over the United States as long as you have your location on. It is *NOT* a tracking device. It also can help you check out if you or someone else has Warrants, you can do background checks on this app, and you can find attorneys and predators in your area.

Responsibilities of a Citizen

As a good citizen, you need to always tell the truth. A person's honesty is all they have when dealing with the judicial system. Some people are never taught how to do the right thing by telling the truth. They have this idea that they need to mind their own business, and if they keep their mouths shut, it will be okay. The truth is, when something happens to your family, you would want someone to tell what happened, right? Therefore, if you know someone committed a crime, you should tell them to turn themselves in.

If You Weren't Taught About Right and Wrong—Stopping the Vicious Cycle

Your natural instinct is to survive, to take what you want and need to survive. But what if no one ever told you what you were doing was wrong? What if no one ever taught you basic survival skills that could change your outcome, skills as simple as fishing so you won't starve? Then you could fish and perhaps sell your fish to make money to survive.

When it comes to the vicious cycle, you have to know right from wrong, and hopefully, someone cares about you enough to tell you when you are doing something wrong. Unfortunately, the government has created so many rules that instinct now can be a crime.

I have a seminar and webinars that I do that address many of the issues in this book. Some of the topics discussed are:

- Knowing and understanding the top reasons people get pulled over

- Why and how people get arrested when they're pulled over

- What flags an officer when they are typing up random plates

- How to not get illegally searched

The purpose of the seminars is to discuss issues that people may need extra help in understanding and communicating, with questions and answers.

Tips for When You're Pulled Over

1. **NEVER FLEE.** You will always get caught and it will only make the situation worse.

2. You need to understand that driving with a suspended license or maybe a bag of marijuana in your car is not worth getting a felony fleeing case.

3. When you know your rights in the first place, they have no right to search your car.

4. **BE NICE, EVEN IF YOU'RE MAD.**

5. Everything is recorded, so don't just start talking or answering questions.

6. Put both hands on the steering wheel.

7. Ask the officer why you were pulled over.

8. **THEN, BE QUIET.**

9. Try not to get tricked into admitting you did something wrong—things like you didn't have your seatbelt on.

10. Make sure your doors are locked.

11. Cracking your window gives them less chance to smell marijuana, so they can't use the fact they smelled marijuana to search your car.

12. If you don't have insurance or the registration, say you misplaced it. Then take the ticket and resolve it later.

13. If they ask to search your car, ask why, then say **YOU DO NOT CONSENT**. You may have to repeat it a few times as they may try bully you.

14. Ask if you're being detained or if you're free to go.

15. If you decide you're going to get out the car: Turn the car off, take the key out the ignition, put the key in your pocket, and ask the officer to step away from your car. Lock the door as you are getting out and shut the door. They still have no right to search you or your car. And, yes, they are trying to think of a reason to get into your car.

    NOTE: If you have keyless operation, make sure you put your key in your pocket before the cop gets to your car. If you're a woman, you don't want to go to reach for your key from your purse, for instance, and the officer mistakes it for something else

16. Don't forget to ask the officer if you're free to go or if you're being detained.

17. If you are arrested and there's a licensed passenger in your vehicle, the police can let them take your vehicle instead of impounding it. Beware: the police like to impound your vehicle so they can do an inventory search. That gives them the right to look through your vehicle. That's their way of getting around a Warrant.

18. If you locked your car when you got out of it, they may just let someone pick it up instead of impounding it.

19. Keep your doors locked because the police may try to open the door without you wanting them to.

20. Don't fall for the set up. If you only roll your window down a little bit, it gives them less reason to say they need to search your car because they claim they smell marijuana, and it's for your own safety. Plus, it shows them you know your rights, and they can't just reach in your car and open your door.

21. The first thing you need to ask the officer is why you were pulled over. *For example,* if they say you were speeding, that only gives them Probable Cause to get your license, registration, and insurance. Nothing else.

22. Ask the officer if you have committed a crime. At this point, the crime is probably only going to get you a

ticket. The officer has no Probable Cause to search you. It's the 4th Amendment.

23. Even if you don't have proof of insurance with you, that doesn't give them the right to search you.

24. There is no legal basis for your passengers to have to give them their identification, even if they ask for it.

25. Most people make the mistake of giving the officer permission to search their car. You do not have to give the officer permission to search your car.

26. There's a difference between permission and Probable Cause. Don't get tricked into letting an officer search your car. Don't give them an opportunity to put something in your car.

27. Also, you do not have to answer any questions. *For example,* if the officer asks where you're going, tell the officer you don't have to answer that.

28. If you're asked to get out the car, you should comply because this is a lawful order. But if you decide not to, say you do not consent, ask for a Warrant, then ask the officer to call his supervisor to the scene.

You Have Rights

A. Never give the police permission to search your car, even if you have nothing in it at all. The police have to show a reason to search and question you, but if you consent, they do not need a reason.

B.   If you consent, you have just given your rights away. Consent is the enemy of your constitutional rights. Don't assume the cops are justified in searching or questioning you so you just agree to give consent. If they were justified, they wouldn't ask for your consent.

C.   Don't be intimidated by the cop telling you it will go easier for you if you give consent. It goes easier for them, not you!

D.   If they want to look through your car, in your purse, in your trunk, etc., **DO NOT GIVE CONSENT!** Do you mind opening your trunk? Open your purse. These are all ways the cops get consent.

E.   The cops will not tell you they need consent to look. They ask for it in sneaky ways so you don't even realize what you just did. They may threaten to arrest you and oand inconvenient, but there is no crime on insisting on your constitutional rights, and there is no crime in not consenting.

F.   Another way to give your rights away: when the police ask you to come in for questioning. This is voluntary. Even if you feel intimidated that you need to go, you don't.

G.   Please know they have no rights unless you are taken into custody and that usually means an arrest.

H. If you start talking to the cops without them asking you a direct question, you have just given your rights up—even if you are in custody!

I. If the cops talk between themselves or to someone else and you overhear them (this is intentional on their part), you may feel the need to chime in. You just gave away your rights, even if you are in custody!

J. **IF YOU WISH TO REMAIN SILENT, YOU MUST REMAIN SILENT! IF YOU TALK, YOU HAVE JUST GIVEN UP YOUR RIGHTS.**

K. If they ask to search your car, even if: (a) you think they will find it or see it, (b) you think you have nothing to hide, (c) you think saying **NO** will get you in more trouble, or (d) worse, you think they'll search no matter what you say, **ALWAYS SAY NO!**

L. The cops may try to coerce you by telling you that you'll get in more trouble by saying no or that it will be harder on you if they have to get a Warrant, etc. If you give your consent, you have just lost your constitutional rights.

M. If you give your consent, the cops don't need Probable Cause to search. If you don't give your consent, then the cops have to give the court a good reason why they searched your vehicle.

N. The same goes for a pat-down search. If a cop sees you on the street, they have to have reasonable suspicion of a crime committed by you. Then, they can only ask your name (you need to tell the truth if you decide to answer) and they can only pat you down for what they can readily feel through your clothing. This is not an invasive search, **UNLESS YOU GIVE THEM CONSENT.**

O. The cops can get away with more than a pat-down if you tell on yourself. If the cop asks what are you carrying and you tell him, then you've just told on yourself. Even if it's something that has nothing to do with the crime the cop had suspicions about in the first place, or if it's something they never would have detected by a pat-down search, you just told on yourself and gave away your rights!

P. You cannot disobey a lawful order from a police officer—*for example,* if the police officer asks you to get out the car. Failure to obey a lawful order is a felony.

Q. You are not going to win a fight with the cops on the street. They have power and force. Be polite and comply with direct orders, but do not give consent if asked. Remain silent. The fight comes later in the courtroom. One ugly charge that can be added to a minor infraction is resisting and obstructing a police officer, which is a felony.

Trials

Before you make any statements or do a deposition (civil cases only), always hire an attorney. Don't tell the police or the attorney who may depose you anything without consulting your attorney. It could come back to haunt you if there is a trial. *AN ATTORNEY CANNOT HELP YOU DURING A DEPOSITION*, but a good, experienced attorney will have an idea of the questions you will be asked and should prepare you for the deposition. *IT MUST BE PROVEN YOU DID SOMETHING WRONG. DON'T HELP THEM BY TALKING TOO MUCH.*

Trial: Criminal Case

Prosecutor: wants you to be guilty and wants to catch you in lies; makes you look like a bad person.

Defense Attorney: wants to show you as innocent of what you were charged with and tell your story in a good way to protect you.

Trial: Civil Case

If you're the one suing, you're the plaintiff. If you're the one being sued, you're the defendant.

Plaintiff's Attorney: wants to prove the plaintiff deserves what they're asking for.

Defense Attorney: wants to make the plaintiff look bad and show they're lying.

In civil cases, in lawsuits against big companies like insurance companies, these companies have deep pockets and they will lie to jurors to make you lose your case. Even if they are a multi-million-dollar company, they will fight you over as little as $25,000, especially if you're from a lower-class area, even when they know they're wrong. Don't trust anyone; they buy people off all the time. Their job is to make their lies look good, and in a lot of cases, the jurors have made a determination that you are guilty before even hearing your case. They are told to only look at the evidence, but unfortunately, if they don't like you, they will make up any reason not to vote in your favor.

If your case goes to trial, a lot of your dirty laundry may come out.

Depositions

Depositions are very important. That is when the opposing attorney questions you and everything you say is recorded. Then, when you get to trial, they try to turn it against you to make you look bad, using your words against you. You will be able to have your attorney there, but they won't be able to really say anything to help you. A good attorney will prepare you for what to expect before the deposition. You should make your answers short and sweet.

If you go to trial, it is important for you to remember everything that has happened. You must pay attention to everything. Take time to read all the depositions because this is what they are going to use against you.

In a criminal case, the prosecutor wants to find you guilty, and your attorney (defense attorney) is supposed to help you. In a civil case, if you are the plaintiff—that's when you are suing someone for something they did to you—your attorney is going to help you explain your story. The defense attorney tries to make you look like a liar, discredit everything you say, and trick you into saying things that may hurt you later. If you are being sued, you are the defendant, and it's the reverse.

Knowing When to Use Your Rights

If you are driving completely legitimately—this means you have a driver's license, proof of insurance, registration, and no Warrants—you have no reason to have an attitude. If you do have something illegal in your car, guess what? The police don't know it and don't have a reason to look for it—*UNLESS YOU DO SOMETHING DUMB!*

You need to comply with the police. Did you hear me? Here is how your stop is supposed to go:

1. *ROLL YOUR WINDOW DOWN.*
   It can be halfway as long as the police can see inside your vehicle for yours and their safety.

2. *"HELLO, OFFICER."*
   Don't fall for the trick of, "Do you know why I'm pulling you over?" The answer is always no!

3. *"CAN YOU TELL ME WHY I'M BEING PULLED OVER?"*
   He responds.

4. If he orders you to get out of the car, you say:
   "YES, OFFICER." ROLL UP YOUR WINDOW, TAKE THE KEY OUT, AND LOCK YOUR DOOR. TALK TO THE OFFICER BECAUSE YOU HAVEN'T DONE ANYTHING WRONG.
   Don't think like a criminal. All law enforcement officers are not out to get you. They're just trying to do their job.

What has been happening is people don't know when an officer gives an order, **YOU MUST FOLLOW THE ORDER OR IT IS BREAKING THE LAW.** That gives them the right to pull you out of the car! If you curse at the officer, it is a misdemeanor and you can get arrested for disorderly conduct, so stop trying to be a tough guy!

This is knowing when to use your rights. By not complying, that makes you **A DUMB CRIMINAL!**

We know it may be harder for certain ethnic people, but stay calm and show respect to the officer. Even if you know he's pulling you over on some bull, don't show any disrespect. If you do, you make yourself a target.

Now that you know when to use your rights, you need to understand if you follow all the rules and they violate you, guess what? Now you can sue them, but make sure *you don't tell* them your plan.

So, when you're pulled over, stop thinking and acting like a criminal by assuming every police officer is bad or having a bad day. Know the difference between a traffic crime and a criminal crime.

What You Can and Cannot Do

When selecting a jury, you have the right to get rid of some jurors you feel wouldn't understand your case. After selection of the jury, you need to pay attention to both attorneys' openings. The opening is when both attorneys explain their version of the case to the judge and jury.

If you get on the stand, you need to understand that you know what happened in your situation, but they don't. To paint the real picture, you may have to speak out of line when asked a question, and it may seem you are upsetting the judge or the other attorney. The point is for the jury to understand you and see what kind of person you are.

In saying that, you must understand, in a civil case, if you are the plaintiff, when the defense attorney asks you a question, they are wanting you to give the answer they want. So, if they ask questions in a confusing way, it's so they can get the answers they want. This is where you have to tell your story. They may want a yes or a no answer, but that may just trap you into looking guilty.

Most jurors don't live in the same world you may live in—you know, the world where crime exists. You may live in an area where the local street kid has to carry a gun to the store just so they don't get robbed on the way there. But the jury may not understand that lifestyle. They may think, well, he was asking for trouble and he needed a gun license. That may be true, but there are a lot of unsafe neighborhoods where people have to do what they have to do to protect themselves.

So, when you're testifying, you need to clearly explain your story, like you're talking to a child. The opposing attorney wants you to look like you're a criminal and a liar. You must know how to explain to the jury what happened without getting mad, without cursing, and without slang. These people are there to judge you. It is very stressful being on the stand, but you must try to stay calm and get your story out.

♣ ♣ ♣

30.   Charge Glossary

First Degree Criminal Sexual Conduct (CSC 1)

• Vaginal, oral, or anal sex, actual insertion, sex with a minor, or sex with the mentally challenged.

• Penalty: Life in a state prison, possible life without parole, possible minimum 25 years, lifetime GPS tether.

• Sex Offender Registration: Lifetime public registration, quarterly reporting.

Second Degree Criminal Sexual Conduct (CSC 2)

• Touching with sexual satisfaction. Rubbing a penis on a clitoris without insertion and ejaculation.

• Penalty: 15 years in a state prison, possible lifetime GPS tether.

• Sex Offender Registration: Lifetime or 25 years public registration, quarterly or semi-annual reporting.

Third Degree Criminal Sexual Conduct (CSC 3)

• Penetration (fingering), possibly consensual but underage.

• Penalty: 15 years in a state prison.

- Sex Offender Registration: Lifetime public registration, quarterly reporting.

Fourth Degree Criminal Sexual Conduct (CSC 4)

- Touching someone in an inappropriate sexual way (grabbing breasts, butt, or crotch).

- Penalty: 2 years in a state prison and/or $500 fine.

- Sex Offender Registration: Lifetime, 25, or 15 years public registration (depending on age of Complainant), quarterly, semi-annual, or annual reporting.

Assault With Intent to Commit Criminal Sexual Conduct Involving Sexual Penetration

- Assault, planning to actually have sex (holding someone down, but not actually finishing).

- Penalty: 10 years in a state prison.

- Sex Offender Registration: Lifetime public registration, quarterly reporting.

Assault With Intent to Commit Criminal Sexual Conduct in the Second Degree

- Assault, planning to orgasm (by masturbation).

- Penalty: 5 years in a state prison.

- Sex Offender Registration: Lifetime, 25, or 15 years public registration (depending on age of Complainant), quarterly, semi-annual, or annual reporting.

Accosting, Enticing, or Soliciting a Child for Immoral Purposes (Accosting a Minor for Immoral Purposes)

- Bribe or make a promise to a child for sex.

- Penalty: 4 years in a state prison and/or $4,000 fine.

- Sex Offender Registration: 25 years public registration, semi-annual reporting.

Gross Indecency

- Sexual acts between the same gender.

- Penalty: 5 years in a state prison and/or $2,500 fine; minimum 1 day in jail and maximum life in a state prison for "sexually delinquent persons".

- Sex Offender Registration: Lifetime or 25 years public registration (depending on ages of Complainant and accused), quarterly or semi-annual reporting.

Child Sexually Abusive Material (and Child Sexually Abusive Activity)

- Child naked pictures or video.

- Penalty: 4, 7, or 20 years in a state prison and/or a $10,000, $50,000, or $100,000 fine, respectively, depending on whether the alleged offense involves knowing possession, distribution, or production of the child sexually abusive material.

- Sex Offender Registration: 25 or 15 years public registration, annual or semi-annual reporting.

Indecent Exposure & Aggravated Indecent Exposure

- Showing your private parts.

- Penalty: 1 year in jail and/or a $1,000 fine (Indecent Exposure); 2 years in a state prison and/or a $2,000 fine (Aggravated Indecent Exposure).

- Sex Offender Registration: Possible 15 years public registration.

Felonious Assault (Assault With a Dangerous Weapon)

- Attacking a person with a weapon.

- Penalty: 4 years in a state prison and/or $2,000 fine.

Assaulting, Resisting, or Obstructing a Police Officer ("Certain Persons")

- Lying to the police, not following the police's directions, or resisting the police.

- Penalty: 2 years in a state prison and/or $2,000 fine.

Felony Domestic Violence, Third Offense

- Injure a spouse or person in same house (most likely your 3rd time).

- Penalty: 5 years in a state prison and/or $5,000 fine.

Assault With Intent to Do Great Bodily Harm ("GBH"), Less Than Murder

- Serious injury causing harm to a person's health.

- Penalty: 10 years in a state prison and/or $5,000 fine.

Assault With Intent to Commit Murder ("AWICM")

- Not just assaulting a person, but trying to kill, not just hurt, a person.

- Penalty: Life in a state prison or any term of years.

Assault With Intent to Commit a Felony (Other Various Types)

- Michigan law has also earmarked certain felonies for special treatment with specific statutes, including even harsher potential punishment. Here are a few examples:

- ◆ Assault With Intent to Commit Armed Robbery: Life in a state prison.

- ◆ Assault With Intent to Commit Unarmed Robbery: 15 years in a state prison.

- ◆ Assault With Intent to Commit Sexual Penetration: 10 years in a state prison.

- ◆ Assault With Intent to Commit Sexual Contact: 5 years in a state prison.

- ◆ Assault With Intent to Maim: 10 years in a state prison.

Stalking

- Always watching someone or always contacting someone who doesn't want to be contacted by you. *You're obsessed!*

- Penalty: 1 year in jail and/or $1,000 fine, or 5 years in a state prison and a $10,000 fine (depending on the circumstances).

Aggravated Stalking

- Threatening and harassing while always watching someone.

- Penalty: 5 years in a state prison and/or $10,000 fine, or 10 years in a state prison and a $15,000 fine (depending on the circumstances).

Domestic Assault, First Offense

- Assaulting someone you're in a relationship with.

- Penalty: 93 days in jail and/or $500 fine.

Domestic Assault, Second Offense

- Second time assaulting someone you're in a relationship with.

- Penalty: 1 year in jail and/or $1,000 fine.

Aggravated Domestic Assault

- Assault of the person you're in a relationship with that would cause serious injury.

- Penalty: 1 year in jail and/or $1,000 fine.

Domestic Assault, Third Offense – Felony

- Third time assaulting a spouse with injury.

- Penalty: 5 years in a state prison and/or $5,000 fine.

First Degree Home Invasion

- Someone breaks into and enters a home with intent to steal or assault; or breaks into and enters a dwelling without permission, and at any time during the breaking and entering, they steal or assault and are armed with a dangerous weapon; or another person is lawfully in the dwelling at the time of the breaking and entering. 20 years.

Second Degree Home Invasion

- Someone breaks into and enters a home with intent to steal or assault; or someone enters without permission to commit felony larceny or assault; or someone breaks into and enters without permission, and during the breaking and entering, commits a felony, larceny, or assault. 15 years.

Third Degree Home Invasion

- Someone breaks into a home with intent to steal. 5 years.

- Someone breaks into and enters a building with intent to commit a misdemeanor in the building, enters without permission with intent to commit a misdemeanor in the building; or breaks into and enters without permission, and during the breaking and entering, commits a misdemeanor. 2-5 years

- Someone breaks into and enters a building without permission, and at any time while entering the building, present in the building, or exiting the building, violates any of the following: an order to protect a person or persons; a probation term or condition; a parole term or condition; a personal protection order term or condition; a bond or bail condition; or a pretrial release condition. 2-5 years

First Degree Retail Fraud (Felony)

- Intent to steal from a store. Jail time of up to 5 years and potential fine of either $10,000 or three times the value of the stolen property, whichever is greater.

Second Degree Retail Fraud (Misdemeanor)

- Jail time of up to 1 year and a potential fine of either $2,000 or three times the value of the stolen property, whichever is greater.

Third Degree Retail Fraud (Misdemeanor)

- Jail time of up to 93 days and a potential fine of either $500 or three times the value of the stolen property, whichever is greater.

Carrying a Concealed Weapon (CCW)

- Carrying a firearm or dangerous weapon (dagger, dirk, razor, stiletto, taser, or knife having a blade over 3 inches in length). 2-5 years.

●●●

31. Disclosure

The information given in this guide is true. The place where the crime may be committed may change because of race or gender. The names of the court processes may slightly change because of the court's location.

The *Criminal Chart* is based on first-time offenses. If you have a criminal record, your guidelines for sentencing will have longer prison times. Also, if you have more than one charge, it changes the guidelines and the punishment may be harsher.

Jails are very expensive. Inmates get charged $75-$200 per day for "3 hots and a cot". So think about that.

Jails charge just as much as a hotel stay, but you didn't ask to stay at their hotel.

This book was created to help you make better choices. **THIS BOOK IS IN NO WAY MEANT TO GIVE OR REPLACE LEGAL ADVICE. THE INFORMATION HEREIN IS PROVIDED TO HELP YOU HELP YOURSELF, AND YOUR ATTORNEY, IF YOU HAPPEN TO GET CAUGHT-UP IN THE SYSTEM!**

If you found this book to be interesting and want additional information, please email me or go to the website and provide your email contact information.

- Website: **www.dontbeadumbasscriminal.com**
- Email: **Dontbeadumbasscriminal@yahoo.com**
- Instagram: **Dontbeadumbasscriminal**
- Facebook: **Dontbeadumbasscriminal**

 For the **BANKS BAIL BONDS** app, go to the **www.banksbailbond.com** site, or your Google Play or iTunes store, type in Banks Bail Bonds, and download it for free. Put your information in, then push the app tutorial button.

If you bought this book in eBook format and would like a print copy, you can buy this book:

- Directly from me:
  www.dontbeadumbasscriminal.com

- On our Facebook page. There is a link to purchase the book.

- Amazon: www.amazon.com

Please like our Facebook page and rate our book.

✹✹✹

Who says crime doesn't pay?
It pays very well—just not for you!

Made in the USA
Columbia, SC
29 November 2019